QUICK GUIDE
TO DATABASE
MANAGEMENT

D1561100

QUICK GUIDE TO DATABASE MANAGEMENT

JEFFREY R. STEWART
Professor of Business Education
Virginia Polytechnic Institute
  and State University
Blacksburg, Virginia

NANCY M. MELESCO
Instructor of Business and Data
  Processing
Ferrum College
Ferrum, Virginia

SANDRA R. McMINNIS
Assistant Professor of Computer Science
Richard Bland College of the College of
  William and Mary
Petersburg, Virginia

Gregg Division/McGRAW-HILL PUBLISHING COMPANY

New York Atlanta Dallas St. Louis San Francisco
Auckland Bogotá Caracas Hamburg Lisbon
London Madrid Mexico Milan Montreal New Delhi
Paris San Juan São Paulo Singapore
Sydney Tokyo Toronto

Sponsoring Editor: Adina Genn
Editing Supervisor: Frances Koblin
Design and Art Supervisor: Joseph Piliero
Production Supervisor: Kathleen Donnelly

Text Designer: b c graphics
Cover Designer: b c graphics

QUICK GUIDE TO DATABASE MANAGEMENT

1 2 3 4 5 6 7 8 9 0   HESHES   8 9 6 5 4 3 2 1 0 9

ISBN 0-07-061504-7

CONTENTS

PREFACE

Quick Guide to Database Management explains database management to new users and serves as a handy reference for experienced users. This book demonstrates how anyone can manage information by using various types of electronic databases.

Quick Guide to Database Management is not a substitute for the vendor's manuals that accompany commercial software packages. Rather, this text is a valuable resource that will help you approach any database management system with confidence.

Chapter 1 discusses what databases are and what they can do. Chapter 2 considers all the elements needed to design a database. Chapter 3 explains how to search for records and update files. Chapter 4 covers how to sort records in ascending or descending order, assemble informal listings of records, and produce a professional report. Chapter 5 describes how to maintain software and hardware, keep data accurate and confidential, and select the software package that best fits your needs.

The database project, at the end of the book, is a series of application exercises that provide you with the opportunity to get practical, office-related experience in database management.

Quick Guide to Database Management is designed to make learning easy. Each chapter begins with a list of objectives. The numerous illustrations and examples clarify important concepts in the text. A vocabulary list at the end of each chapter helps you master the definitions of key terms. The glossary at the end provides definitions. A self-check review, following the vocabulary list, quizzes you on the content of each chapter with multiple choice, true and false, and short-answer questions.

Upon completing *Quick Guide to Database Management*, you will be prepared to contribute to the planning, design, maintenance and integration of databases. You will also be able to make educated decisions in selecting appropriate software.

Jeffrey R. Stewart
Nancy M. Melesco
Sandra R. McMinnis

CHAPTER 1: UNDERSTANDING DATABASES

In Chapter 1 you will:

- Recognize the power of a database.
- Distinguish between data and information.
- Consider what is needed to set up a database.
- Identify the components of a database.
- Distinguish among hierarchical, network, and relational databases.

THE POWER OF A DATABASE

Massive amounts of raw facts, or data, are used to produce information for effective decision making in business, industry, government, and even the home. But data must be organized before it

This executive uses a computer database to organize, access, and retrieve information.

can be used. One way to organize data is through the use of a computer database. A *database* is an orderly, usually very large, body of data which allows you to process, access, and retrieve information.

A computer database provides powerful means of organizing data and accessing information. The following case illustrates the power of a database.

Todd Daniels is the secretary of the Ski Club in his city. When he first joined the club 10 years ago, it had only 30 active members. The club was originally established for those who had an interest in taking skiing trips at group rates. Over the years the Ski Club evolved into a social club, with a large number of members having a variety of interests other than skiing.

In addition to skiing, members play tennis and golf, take trips, have parties, and engage in numerous leisure-time activities. Todd has the task of sending mailings to all the members each month. He also works with the program director in planning activities. In doing so, it is necessary to take into consideration the members' interests.

There have been some complaints during the last few months about the number and quality of the programs offered. Therefore, Todd has decided to send each member a questionnaire. The questionnaire will ask for the following: member's name, address, occupation, birthdate, work and home phone numbers, interests, and names and ages of family members.

Todd plans to enter this data into a database using his microcomputer and a purchased database software package. Once the database is established, he will be able to:

1. Print mailing labels for the notices he sends to members each month.
2. Query (ask a question of) the file to determine how many members have a certain interest.
3. Sort the file by interest to provide information for program planning.

Each summer the club has a family picnic. Todd and the program director are responsible for planning activities for the children. By knowing the ages of the children and being able to get a count of each age group, they can better plan activities appropriate for everyone. Also, Todd likes to be able to send birthday cards to members from the club. Having this information in a database makes it easy to keep track of everyone's special date.

After hearing of Todd's plans, the club treasurer asked Todd to include in the database the amount of dues each member has paid and the date of last payment.

```
                        THE SKI CLUB

                   MEMBERSHIP QUESTIONNAIRE


     MEMBER'S DATA                      SPOUSE'S DATA


     NAME _____       NAME _____

     ADDRESS _____

     _____


     OCCUPATION _____        OCCUPATION _____

     BIRTHDATE _____/_____/_____      BIRTHDATE _____/_____/_____

     WORK PHONE NUMBER _____        WORK PHONE NUMBER _____

     HOME PHONE NUMBER _____

     INTERESTS (Please check all that apply.)

     _____ Hand/racquetball             _____ Hand/racquetball
     _____ Tennis                       _____ Tennis
     _____ Golf                         _____ Golf
     _____ Travel                       _____ Travel
     _____ Parties                      _____ Parties
     _____ Dancing:  rock               _____ Dancing:  rock
     _____ Dancing:  swing              _____ Dancing:  swing
     _____ Dancing:  folk/square        _____ Dancing:  folk/square
     _____ Cards (bridge)               _____ Cards (bridge)
     _____ Exercise                     _____ Exercise
     _____ Hiking                       _____ Hiking

     OTHER INTERESTS (Please list.)


     _____            _____

     _____            _____

     _____            _____

     _____            _____


     OTHER FAMILY MEMBERS               AGE

     _____            _____

     _____            _____

     _____            _____

     _____            _____
```

Todd uses this questionnaire to collect data from club members.

With a database, Todd can easily print mailing labels whenever necessary.

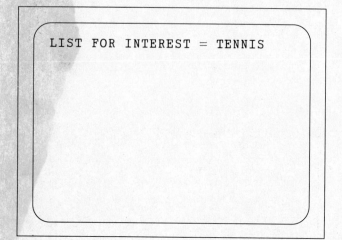

Todd queries the database to find out which members play tennis.

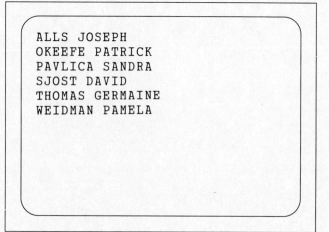

The result of the query is a list of the members who checked tennis on the questionnaire.

Dues are $30 a year and are payable on the anniversary date of enrollment. Dues can be paid in a lump sum, in two installments of $15 each, or in three installments of $10 each. With that information in the computer, the treasurer can easily keep track of the amount each member owes.

Todd and the program director are confident that the complaints about the programs and activities will quickly change to compliments.

DATA VERSUS INFORMATION

You have seen how a computer database might be used by a club or other organization. Computers are also found in the home and in every kind of business—from the small "Mom and Pop" store to the giant corporation. Computers organize and synthesize data to provide the information a business needs for survival. *Data* consist of raw facts that are fed into a computer to be processed.

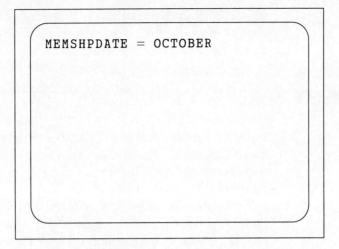

The treasurer queries the database to get a list of the members to bill for dues this month.

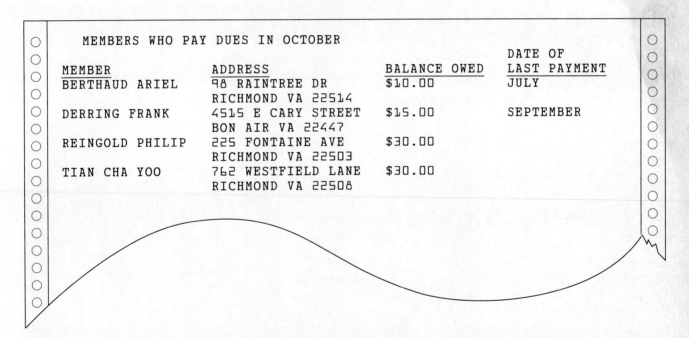

```
   MEMBERS WHO PAY DUES IN OCTOBER
                                                        DATE OF
   MEMBER               ADDRESS            BALANCE OWED  LAST PAYMENT
   BERTHAUD ARIEL       98 RAINTREE DR     $10.00        JULY
                        RICHMOND VA 22514
   DERRING FRANK        4515 E CARY STREET $15.00        SEPTEMBER
                        BON AIR VA 22447
   REINGOLD PHILIP      225 FONTAINE AVE   $30.00
                        RICHMOND VA 22503
   TIAN CHA YOO         762 WESTFIELD LANE $30.00
                        RICHMOND VA 22508
```

The treasurer then obtains a printout showing their names, addresses, account balances, and dates of last payment.

For example, an airline ticket has different sections, including date, time, and point of departure; date, time, and point of arrival; and price of the ticket. To both the traveler and the airline, each separate raw fact, by itself, is of little value. Combined, these data become important *information*. The traveler can use this information to plan an itinerary. By entering this ticket information into a database, the airline can quickly determine seating availability on each flight and which flights are the most profitable. Information is one of the most valuable assets of an organization, and databases are an important way to produce information.

WHAT YOU NEED TO SET UP A DATABASE

There are two requirements for the creation of a database. The first is a *database management system (DBMS)*. A DBMS is a computer program (software package) that allows you to create and use a database. Database software packages range widely in price and complexity. Chapter 5 discusses the selection of database software for your needs.

Through a DBMS, data can be added to or deleted from a database, changed, sorted, searched for, retrieved, and printed. Many DBMSs allow calculations to be done and graphs to be drawn.

A second requirement for creating a database is a proper database design. The important question to ask is, "Who is going to use the database and for what purposes?" Employees of a company have different uses for the company's data. For example, a sales manager uses the data to determine the numbers and amounts of sales, whereas the chief accountant uses some of the same data to determine the income and expenses of the company. The data-

These are a few database software packages used today.

base should be designed so that data needed by all employees are included. The data must be entered in an efficient way in order to be conveniently accessed and easily understood by all who will use them.

COMPONENTS OF A DATABASE

The smallest component of a database is a *field*, which is a category of data. If in a database you were to store information on a particular product, you might have a different field for the product code, product description, unit cost, and percent of markup. The vertical columns in the database represent fields. Together, the fields make up a record.

Product Code Field	Product Description Field	Unit Cost Field	Markup Field
B1078	EXTENSION CORD	00125	12000

Each of the above *fields* contains one item of data. Note that the Markup field is a percentage in which 12000 is understood to be 120.00 percent.

A *record* is a cluster of information in a database representing a person, product, or other unit. An example of a record is the information in a database on a particular customer. Another example might be the information on a product, such as an extension cord. The horizontal rows in a database are records. Collectively, these records make up a file.

Product Code	Product Description	Unit Cost	Percent of Markup
B1078	EXTENSION CORD	00125	12000

Record

This *record* from the product file is made up of pieces of data that all describe one product—extension cord.

In a *file*, all the related records are handled as one unit. The files themselves are interrelated. For example, a database used in a hardware store might include several files, such as a customer file, an accounts receivable file, and a product file. These interrelated files make up a database.

Customer File

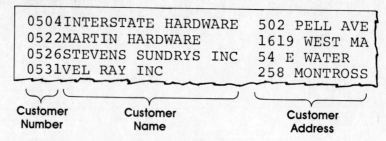

Customer   Customer   Customer
Number   Name   Address

Accounts Receivable File

Customer Product Quantity Price of
Number   Code   Each Item

Product File

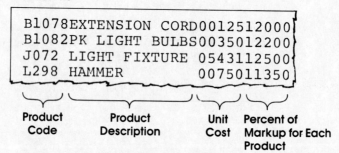

Product   Product   Unit   Percent of
Code   Description   Cost Markup for Each
                                       Product

Note: The different files are interrelated, thereby making up a database. Also note that each file consists of several records and each record contains fields.

FIELD TYPES

When you design a database and are categorizing data into fields, you must assign a name to each field and determine the field length and field type. Field types include numeric, alphanumeric, logical, date, and memo.

Numeric fields contain digits (0–9) or a combination of digits (for example, 25). Numeric fields may also contain a decimal point (1259.98) and a minus sign (−254.87). If a calculation is to be made using the content of a field, the field must be defined as numeric. Note that when a numeric field contains a positive value, no sign is used because it is understood to be positive.

COMPONENTS OF A DATABASE

Component	Definition	Examples
Field	*One* data unit about a person or an item	1. One customer's address: 1619 West Maryland Ave. 2. One customer's name: Interstate Hardware
Record	*Several* individual units of data (fields) about one person or item	Record of one customer: 0504 Interstate Hardware 502 Pell Ave.
File	A *group* of like records	File of all customers: Interstate Hardware Martin Hardware Stevens Sundrys Inc. Vel-Ray Inc.
Database	A *collection of related* files organized to fit the information needs of the user	Customer file Accounts receivable file Product file

Alphanumeric or character fields may contain any character—a letter of the alphabet, a digit (0–9), or any symbol or punctuation mark. Alphanumeric fields may contain characters in any combination. For example, a social security number field containing 223–77–6650 is an alphanumeric field for two reasons: hyphens are included with the digits and social security numbers are not used in calculations. A name field is always alphanumeric because it contains letters of the alphabet. An amount expressed as #6024 is alphanumeric because it contains the number symbol. What type of fields are (804)555–3721 and − 295.67?

A *logical* field is one that may contain only a true/false or yes/no response. The data are keyed T or F, or Y or N, as in the field titled UNION MEMBER (Y/N).

A *date* field is formatted as shown in the examples below. Some database software supplies the two /'s, so the user keys only the digits in the date. As you can see in the table below, May 21, 1989, can be entered in one of two formats.

MM/DD/YY   *YY/MM/DD*

05/21/89   89/05/21
                   Used when the sorting of
                   dates is required.

A *memo* field is a miscellaneous field in which the user can store information that is unique to a particular record. For example, in the client address database of an accounting firm, a user might indicate the name of the client's spouse, if the client is retired, or if the client was referred by someone.

```
SMITH ANN           52 MAIN STREET   ELMSFORD  NY 12202 RETIRED
WILSON JR           98 EAST ROAD     DURHAM    NY 11917 LISA
RODRIGUEZ LOUIS      7 CIRCLE DRIVE  OAKSDALE  NJ 07988 REFERRED BY A SMITH
```

Memo fields can also be used to indicate the physical location of relevant paperwork that pertains to a particular record.

The length of a field is the maximum number of characters and spaces that may be keyed into the field. A name field might be designed for 22 characters. Most names contain fewer than 22 characters, but a name taking more than 22 characters will not fit into the field. For example, the name JoAnn May takes only 9 characters and spaces. The remaining 13 positions of the field are empty. The name Murray Oil Distributors takes 23 characters and spaces. Therefore, only the first 22 characters can be keyed into the field; the final *s* in Distributors is cut off, or *truncated*. In a numeric field, zeros will be filled in at the left if the number is shorter than the field; truncation will occur on the left if the number is longer.

Names: JoAnn May
Murray Oil Distributors

J	O	A	N	N		M	A	Y													
M	U	R	R	A	Y		O	I	L		D	I	S	T	R	I	B	U	T	O	R

In an alphanumeric field of 22 characters, a name that is shorter than the field will be followed by blanks, as shown in the first line. A name that is longer than the field will be *truncated,* or cut off at the right, as shown in the second line.

Numbers: 2,947
4,523,876

0	0	2	9	4	7
5	2	3	8	7	6

A numeric field, on the other hand, will be filled in with zeros at the left if the number of digits in the field is less than the field length, as shown in the first line. If the number of digits is greater than the field length, *truncation* will also occur on the left, as shown in the second line.

When you create a database file, you must give it an appropriate name, or *filename*. Many DBMSs limit you to only a few characters, such as 8, for a filename. It is important that you carefully choose a name that is symbolic or descriptive of the file. You will learn more about assigning filenames in Chapter 2.

ORGANIZATION OF DATABASES

Databases can be organized in different ways. Information can be stored in a database using one of three models—relational, hierarchical, or network.

The *relational* database model is most often used with the microcomputer because it lends itself well to a relatively small volume of data. With this model, each record in the database must have a fixed length. Within all records of a file, the size of each field must be consistent. The organizing structure of this database sets up relationships between records. Data organized in a table of rows and columns are utilized in this model. You can access a record by using one of several keys. For example, you can retrieve a customer's name by keying a customer's number, or you can key a customer's name in order to find the customer's number. The primary advantage of the relational database model is its simplicity.

The *hierarchical* database model is found most often in large computer systems. This model arranges data by identifying each piece of data and defining the relationships among each of the pieces. The structure of a hierarchical database resembles an organization chart and is often referred to as a tree structure.

The *network* database model has a very complex structure. This model is similar to the hierarchical database model in that it is used most often with large computer systems. The advantage of both models is speed and efficiency of use.

VOCABULARY

alphanumeric field

data

database

database management system (DBMS)

date field

field

file

filename

hierarchical database model

information

logical field

memo field

network database model

numeric field

record

relational database model

truncate

CHAPTER 1
SELF-CHECK REVIEW

TRUE OR FALSE

Identify each statement as true or false by circling T or F. Check your answers on page 101 when you have finished.

1. Information is an asset that is valuable to a company. **T** **F**

2. Data are facts that have been processed into a form that is useful to management in making decisions about the company. **T** **F**

3. A field consists of several records. **T** **F**

4. A DBMS enables users to create a database. **T** **F**

5. If employee data in a database include the department in which each employee works, it is possible to search for and retrieve the records of all employees who work in a particular department. **T** **F**

6. An inventory file would include a record for each item of stock the company sells. **T** **F**

7. A numeric field may contain digits, a number sign (#), and a decimal point. **T** **F**

8. The field REORDER POINT, containing the data 02000, is an example of a logical field. **T** **F**

9. Dates are typically entered into a date field as Month dd, yyyy (January 15, 1991). **T** **F**

10. A relational database model is appropriate for handling a small volume of data. **T** **F**

11. If a field for employee number has been designated as a three-character numeric field, the number of the 1000th employee (with employee number 1000) will be truncated to 000. **T** **F**

MULTIPLE CHOICE

For each statement, select the best choice and write the letter of your choice in the blank. Check your answers on page 101 when you have finished.

1. In order to use a computer database to organize facts into useful information, you need the following:
   a. a computer and a questionnaire
   b. a computer, printer, and memo field
   c. a computer, a DBMS, and a proper database design
   d. fields, records, characters, and files 1. ____

2. Data are
   a. raw facts that are put into the computer
   b. organized and useful in making important business decisions
   c. made up of symbols and letters
   d. assets to the company   2. _____

3. A school's student database contains the following fields: date of enrollment, student major, grade point average, anticipated date of graduation. Searching this database would not
   a. give you quick access to all students with a grade point average of 3.0 or higher
   b. tell you the best format to use in entering the student's date of enrollment
   c. allow you to select all students who plan to graduate next year
   d. allow you to list all business computer majors   3. _____

4. A database consists of
   a. fields which are divided into records
   b. files which are made up of fields containing records
   c. files which contain fields
   d. files made up of records containing fields   4. _____

5. Capabilities of a database management system do not include
   a. sorting records
   b. searching for a particular record
   c. designing the database
   d. printing selected records   5. _____

6. In a computer database, an employee's name, social security number, city, state, ZIP Code, and phone number are parts of an employee
   a. record
   b. field
   c. data sheet
   d. folder   6. _____

7. Which of the following is an example of a numeric field?
   a. (804) 555–1238
   b. −446.78
   c. 446 Main St.
   d. #7214   7. _____

8. Which of the following is an example of an alphanumeric field?
   a. 2898 W. Fifth Avenue
   b. .24
   c. −200.45
   d. 4365   8. _____

9. Which of the following is not an example of a logical field?

Field Name	Value	
a. ON RDA REPORT?	Y/N	
b. MEMBER FBLA/PBL?	Y/N	
c. EMPLOYED < 10 YRS?	T/F	
d. CREDIT RATING	EX/POOR	9. ____

10. What type of database allows you to enter a phone number to find the customer's name or the name to find the customer's phone number?
   a. hierarchical
   b. network
   c. relational
   d. both network and relational   10. ____

CHAPTER 2: FILE PLANNING AND RECORD LAYOUT

In Chapter 2 you will:

- Explore the logical and physical views for planning databases.
- Consider the selection of filenames and key fields.
- Determine how field names are assigned.
- Distinguish among the types of fields.
- Assess procedures for entering data, proofreading, and documenting.

In Chapter 1 you learned what a database is and how information in a database is organized. You learned that you must have software and a design in order to create a database. In this chapter you will learn how to design a database according to the kind of information it will manage and how it will be used.

LOGICAL VIEW

The first consideration in planning a database is to determine how people in your organization might use the information in the database. How users view the data is called the *logical view*. Each user is concerned with the way the data relate to his or her own job. For example, workers in the Payroll Department view employee data in terms of the number of hours worked and the rate of pay of each employee. People in the Human Resources Department are also interested in employee pay but not in details about number of hours worked. They are more interested in keeping track of who does what job in what department, what the basic salaries or wages are for different types of jobs, and what job vacancies need to be filled.

The person designing the database must be aware of the needs of all users. This will help to ensure that the necessary data will be included and that the database will be effective and useful for everyone.

To illustrate how people view data differently depending on the function they perform in an organization, consider this example. Pierce Business Forms, a manufacturer of standard forms—such as purchase orders and invoices, all of which are used by small businesses—has a computerized customer file that is used by the Marketing Department, the Accounting Department, and the Shipping Department. How the director of each department views the data in the customer file is shown in the table below.

PHYSICAL VIEW

Having considered the logical view of a database and having recognized the needs of all users, you can direct your attention to the *physical view*—how the data are actually arranged in the database. This means planning what fields are to be included in the records and how the fields are to be named and arranged.

DATABASE FILE DESIGN

The design of a database includes the following activities:

1. Selecting the name of the file, or the filename.
2. Selecting key fields.
3. Selecting additional fields.
4. Choosing names for the fields.
5. Determining the type of each field.
6. Determining the sequence of fields.
7. Documenting the database design.

THE LOGICAL VIEW

Marketing Director Marian Sloan's view	Name of customer (business name) Address of customer (mailing address) Phone number of customer Name of the principal contact within the business Types of forms normally ordered Quantities of forms normally ordered Customer's credit rating
Accounting Director Shad Berkowitz's view	Name of customer (business name) Address of customer (mailing address) Quantity of forms ordered (for billing) Prices of forms ordered (for billing) Previous balance due Credit rating Credit terms Amount due
Shipping Director Leslie Powell's view	Name of customer Ship-to address Types of forms ordered (for filling the order) Quantity of each form type ordered

SELECTING THE FILENAME

When creating a file, the first step is to name it. Some database software requires that filenames be limited to eight characters and that the first character be a letter of the alphabet. Usually a filename must consist of letters and/or numbers, with no spaces or special characters. It is wise to choose a name that identifies the file so that you can recognize it easily later. For example, a good name for an employee file might be EMPLOYEE; for a vendor file, VENDOR. These names are *self-documenting*, which means that the names identify the file.

SELECTING KEY FIELDS

Every database file must have one or more key fields. A *key field* is a field whose content is unique for each record in the file; thus it serves as an identifier for the record. For example, an employee file contains the employee's name, address, social security number, department, rate of pay, number of deductions, and tax filing status. Although it is possible for two or more employees to have the same name, every employee has a different social security number. Therefore, the SOCIAL SECURITY NUMBER field is the key field—the field that is unique for each employee.

Just as the social security number is a natural key field for an employee file, it is also a natural key field for a state's transportation agency database of licensed drivers. But in some databases for which there is no natural key field, it is necessary to create one. Note in the illustration on page 18 that the customer order form of Pierce Business Forms has a CUSTOMER NUMBER field. A unique number is assigned to each customer for use as a key field.

The most important consideration in establishing a key field is to be certain that there are no duplicates from one record to another. Using the name of a person or business for a key field in a small database might be satisfactory because of the small chance of duplication. However, in most large databases the possibility of duplication of names precludes their use as key fields. When designing an equipment inventory database, the manufacturer's serial number of each item might seem to be a good choice for the key field. But it is possible in a large database that two manufacturers will have the same serial number on different pieces of equipment. So a safer practice is to assign an inventory number to each item.

In a database for a video rental club, a membership number is usually assigned and a card bearing the number is issued to the member. This number is the primary key. The *primary key* is the key field that is consulted first when retrieving a record. Anyone in the member's household may rent movies using the card bearing the membership number. If a family member forgets the card and does not know the membership number, the store can find the

Pierce Business Forms

CUSTOMER ORDER FORM

Customer
Number ☐☐☐☐☐☐   Phone
                         Number ☐☐ ☐☐☐-☐☐☐☐

Company Name ☐☐☐☐☐☐☐☐☐☐☐☐☐☐☐☐☐☐☐☐☐☐☐☐☐☐☐☐☐☐☐☐

Address ☐☐☐☐☐☐☐☐☐☐☐☐☐☐☐☐☐☐☐☐☐☐☐☐☐☐☐☐☐☐☐☐☐☐☐

☐☐☐☐☐☐☐☐☐☐☐☐☐☐☐☐☐☐☐☐☐☐☐☐☐☐☐☐☐☐☐☐☐☐☐☐

City ☐☐☐☐☐☐☐☐☐☐☐☐☐☐☐☐☐ State ☐☐ ZIP ☐☐☐☐☐-☐☐☐☐

Contact
Person ☐☐☐☐☐☐☐☐☐☐☐☐☐☐☐☐☐☐☐☐☐☐☐☐☐☐ Terms ☐☐☐☐

Ship To
Address ☐☐☐☐☐☐☐☐☐☐☐☐☐☐☐☐☐☐☐☐☐☐☐☐☐☐☐☐☐☐☐☐☐☐☐

☐☐☐☐☐☐☐☐☐☐☐☐☐☐☐☐☐☐☐☐☐☐☐☐☐☐☐☐☐☐☐☐☐☐☐☐

City ☐☐☐☐☐☐☐☐☐☐☐☐☐☐☐☐☐ State ☐☐ ZIP ☐☐☐☐☐-☐☐☐☐

Stock Number	Description	Quantity	Price
		TOTAL	

Source document for data entry. The salesperson fills in the order form when taking
an order from a customer. If the customer is new, the customer number will be
assigned later.

Note: Information about the customer's credit rating and balance due does not
appear on the order form.

customer's account information using the customer's name or home
phone number. These are used as secondary keys to verify membership. A *secondary key* is used to retrieve a record only when
the primary key is not known.

SELECTING ADDITIONAL FIELDS

Once the key field has been chosen, it is necessary to decide what additional fields to include in each record. Only information that is necessary to the operation being performed should be included in the additional fields.

CHOOSING FIELD NAMES

The persons developing the database will select names (or titles) for the fields, and there may not be agreement as to what the names should be. Of most importance is consistency. For example, you might prefix each of several inventory field names with INV, each of the payroll field names with PAY, each of the employee field names with EMP, and each of the customer fields with C or CUST.

Some databases allow only 8 to 12 characters for a field name—a letter followed by other letters and/or numbers—with no spaces or special characters. In those databases, the field name must be brief, yet as descriptive as possible. A name that is not descriptive is easily forgotten. Be consistent when selecting field names so that the names can be easily recognized later. For example, as shown in the table below, the suffix SSNO is used in the field names in all the files that contain a person's social security number. This table provides examples of field names in a database requiring 10 or fewer characters.

Field Names	Field Contents
INVSTOCKNO	(inventory file) stock number
INVNAME	(inventory file) item name
EMPSSNO	(employee file) social security number
CUSTSSNO	(customer file) social security number
PAYPERIOD	(payroll file) pay periods
PAYRATE	(payroll file) rate of pay
CUSTNO	(customer file) customer number

CODED FIELDS

Some database entries are *coded*, which means entered in a very brief form. The use of codes is an important part of database management because it makes data entry quick and easy. Furthermore, records require less space when fields are coded. When space is saved in the creation of records, more records can be kept in the file and you will be less concerned about the space limitations of your disk. Examples of coded fields are the words *full-time student* coded as F and *part-time student* coded as P. Several other codes appear in the table on page 20.

Field	Typical Code	Meaning
CREDIT RATING	E	Excellent
	G	Good
	F	Fair
	P	Poor
STUDENT GRADE LEVEL IN SCHOOL	1	Freshman
	2	Sophomore
	3	Junior
	4	Senior
MARITAL STATUS	D	Divorced
	M	Married
	S	Single
	W	Widowed
RACE	A	Asian
	B	Black
	C	Caucasian
	H	Hispanic

DETERMINING FIELD TYPES

You learned about field types in Chapter 1. Not all databases require that you declare a field to be either alphanumeric or numeric, but it is important that the file designer and the person entering the data know the type. This way there is less likely to be an error in entering data that must be numeric for calculations. The field types, their definitions, and examples of each are given in the table below.

Field Type	Definition	Examples
Alphanumeric	A field that may contain any combination of letters, numbers, special characters, or spaces.	121 Main St. O'Dell, George 223–68–7880 $45,678.96
Numeric	A field that may contain only digits, a decimal point, and a minus sign. Only fields designated as numeric can be used for arithmetic.	45678.96 −397.24 345
Logical	A field that can contain T or F (TRUE or FALSE) or Y or N (YES or NO).	Y or N for discount allowed
Date	An eight-character field in the format MM/DD/YY or YY/MM/DD used for dates where MM = month, DD = day, and YY = year.*	02/24/89 89/02/24
Memo or other	**A field of any length which allows you to put remarks to annotate records in your database.	Warranty is in vault (note about the location of paperwork that is relevant to this particular record).

* Note: The month and day must always be two digits. For example, February 2, 1989, is coded as 02/02/89.

** Not found in all types of DBMS packages.

DETERMINING THE SEQUENCE OF FIELDS

Arrangement of fields is important so that the data can be keyed quickly and easily. Most data will be entered into a database from original or *source documents*. These contain the data that, when entered, are converted into a form that is read by a computer. Examples of source documents are sales receipts, employee forms, and packing slips. The database fields should be arranged in the same order as the information on the source document. Thus mistakes caused by skipping around are avoided. An example of one of the source documents for Pierce Business Forms is their customer order form, shown below and also on page 18.

This document is an order form which is filled in by the salesperson when taking a customer's order. It takes into account the logical view of the data, incorporating all the data needed by the various users. Note that the AMOUNT DUE, PREVIOUS BALANCE, and CREDIT RATING do not appear on the order form; these fields will be updated in the database after the order is taken. The order

Pierce Business Forms

CUSTOMER ORDER FORM

Customer Number

Phone Number

Company Name

Address

City   State   ZIP

Contact Person   Terms

Ship To Address

City   State   ZIP

Stock Number | Description | Quantity | Price

TOTAL

Source document for data entry.

form includes the assigned key field, the CUSTOMER NUMBER. Using the order form, the database record is designed. Shown next are two ways that the record might appear on the computer screen after being designed and before data are entered. How database information appears on the computer screen depends upon what brand of software you are using. Two formats that are in common use are the *columnar screen* format and the *document screen* format. The illustration below shows a columnar database screen, in which field names are aligned in a column at the left. The illustration on page 23 shows a document screen in which field names appear in positions more closely resembling the source document—in this case the customer order form.

```
RECORD NO   1
CCUSTNO:
CPHONENO: (    )    -
CCUSTNAME:
CADDRESS1:
CADDRESS2:
CCITY:
CSTATE:
CZIP:
CCONTACT:
CTERMS:
CSHPADDR1:
CSHPADDR2:
CSHPCITY:
CSHPSTATE:
CSHPZIP:
CSTNO:
CDESCR:
CQUANTITY:
CPRICE:
CAMTDUE:
CPREVBAL:
CCRRATING:
```

Columnar database screen.

```
CCUSTNO:                    CPHONE:

CCUSTNAME:

CADDRESS1:
CADDRESS2:

CCITY:                      CSTATE:        CZIP:

CCONTACT:                   CTERMS:

CSHPADDR1:
CSHPADDR2:
CSHPCITY:                   CSHPSTATE:     CSHPZIP:

CSTNO:

CDESCR:

CQUANTITY:                  CPRICE:

CAMTDUE:

CPREVBAL:                   CCRRATING:

        RECORD NO    1
```

Document screen.

DOCUMENTING THE DATABASE DESIGN

After a database is created, it must be documented by the designer to provide users with operating instructions. In this instance, *documentation* refers to a *hard copy* (paper printout) of the database design that is saved by the user for reference. A sample documentation form appears on page 24. Documentation can also refer to the vendor manuals that accompany commercial software.

RECORD ENTRY

When entering data into a database, you should key it carefully from the source document. Sometimes it is necessary to translate the data on the source document into their coded form. For example, when a source document has *full-time* or *part-time* with one circled, you will key only the letter F or P. If the source document has *Excellent* checked for credit rating, you will translate it to an E, which is one of the credit rating codes.

```
  ○   TITLE OF DATABASE: PAYROLL                                    ○
  ○   CREATOR: IRMA ROSENFELD                                       ○
  ○   DATA CREATED: 04/18/90                                        ○
  ○                                                                 ○
  ○   PRIMARY KEY: SOCSECNO                                         ○
  ○   SECONDARY KEYS:                                               ○
  ○   FIELD NAME      TYPE    LENGTH   NO. DECIMAL PLACES  EXPLANATION  ○
  ○     Name          A       20                           Name of employee  ○
  ○                                                        Last, First, M.I.  ○
  ○     SOCSECNO      A       11                           nnn-nn-nnnn  ○
  ○     PAYRATE       N        5              2                       ○
  ○     HOURSWKD      N        2              0                       ○
  ○     PROFITSHAR    L        1                           Y if employee  ○
  ○                                                        participates in  ○
  ○                                                        company's profit  ○
  ○                                                        sharing plan  ○
  ○                                                                 ○
  ○   INSTRUCTIONS FOR USING FILE: (Any special instructions   ○
  ○     for users should be written here. Also, any coded      ○
  ○     fields used in the file should be described here.)     ○
  ○                                                                 ○
  ○   AUTHORIZED USERS: (List names or titles of those authorized to use  ○
  ○   this file.)                                                  ○
  ○                                                                 ○
  ○   FILE PASSWORD: (Might be listed here unless this is       ○
  ○     secret.)                                                   ○
  ○                                                                 ○
  ○   SCHEDULED BACKUP DATES: (List dates or time periods       ○
  ○     for backing up database file.)                             ○
  ○                                                                 ○
  ○   A SAMPLE SOURCE DOCUMENT IS ATTACHED.                        ○
```

Documentation for the database.

When entering data, be consistent in using uppercase or lowercase letters. Most American computers process data in electronic form using the ASCII code. *ASCII* are the initials for American Standard Code for Information Interchange. The ASCII code for an uppercase letter (K) is different from its lowercase counterpart (k). Therefore, records may not be alphabetized correctly unless they are keyed consistently.

After data for one record have been keyed and before you go to the next record, it is very important that you proofread the data on the screen. The illustration on page 25 is of a document formatted screen which has been filled in and is ready for proofreading. Do you note any obvious errors?

After you have entered all of the records, you should print a hard-copy listing of the entire file. From the hard copy, someone

```
CCUSTNO:  41560              CPHONE:  (804) 894-267

CCUSTNAME:  ROSCOE MANUFACTURING INC

CADDRESS1:  1715 BAY SHORE DRIVE

CADDRESS2:

CCITY:  NORFOLK          CSTATE:  VA    CZIP:  20301-4456

CCONTACT:  ROSCOE GERMAINE      CTERMS:  2/10

CSHPADDR1:  SAME AS ABOVE
CSHPADDR2:
CSHPCITY:                      CSHPSTATE:           CSHPZIP:

CSTNO:  23

CDESCR:  INVOICES

CQUANTITY:  2500          CPRICE:  .25

CAMTDUE:  625.00

CPREVBAL:  550.00      CCRRATING:  E
                RECORD NO    1
```

Sample source document.

must proofread each record carefully. An error can cause multiple problems when using the file. A common problem is that amounts are often keyed incorrectly. It is very easy to key one too many or too few zeros or to transpose (switch) figures.

VOCABULARY

ASCII

coded field

columnar screen

document screen

documentation

hard copy

key field

logical view

physical view

primary key

secondary key

self-documenting

source documents

CHAPTER 2
SELF-CHECK REVIEW

TRUE OR FALSE

Identify each of the following statements as true or false by circling T or F. Check your answers on page 101 when you have finished.

1. When planning your database, it is very important to consider what data each user needs.   T   F

2. Fields in a database should be arranged in the same order as they appear on the source document.   T   F

3. A UNION MEMBERSHIP field in a personnel file would be classified as a numeric field if its contents will contain the character (Y) for yes or the character (N) for no.   T   F

4. The date 5/5/89 in a field has been keyed correctly.   T   F

5. A field containing a Y, indicating that an applicant is a veteran, or an N, indicating that an applicant had no military service, is an example of a logical field.   T   F

6. The data contained in a database field are logically viewed in the same manner by separate departments within the same organization.   T   F

7. In choosing a key field for a file, the most important consideration is the location of the data on the source document.   T   F

8. Data are usually entered into a computer file from a source document.   T   F

9. For some database software, there is a limit on the length of field names.   T   F

10. When naming fields and files, it is best to use names that can be easily recognized by the user.   T   F

11. Because database management systems easily allow listing of records after data entry, it is not necessary to proofread each record as it is entered.   T   F

12. When entering records into a database, being consistent in using uppercase and lowercase letters is not important because the computer considers them the same.   T   F

MULTIPLE CHOICE

For each statement, select the best choice and write the letter of your choice in the blank. Check your answers on page 101 when you have finished.

1. For an employee record, which is the best choice for the key field?
   a. employee name
   b. social security number
   c. rate of pay
   d. department   1. _____

2. For an inventory record, which is the best choice for the key field?
   a. part description
   b. vendor number
   c. manufacturer's serial number
   d. an assigned inventory number   2. _____

3. Which is the best filename for a file of patients' records in a doctor's office?
   a. PATRECFILE
   b. PATIENT
   c. PATINFO
   d. PFILE   3. _____

4. Which is the best field name for recording customer payments if there is another field for recording payments to vendors?
   a. CUSFILE
   b. CUSPMT
   c. VENPMT
   d. PAYMENT   4. _____

5. An example of a source document is
   a. a document screen
   b. an inventory number
   c. a columnar database screen
   d. a packing slip   5. _____

6. Which is an example of numeric data?
   a. #395,754.24
   b. 286#
   c. −7682.92
   d. (619) 555–8934   6. _____

7. Which is an example of a logical field name?
   a. MALE OR FEMALE
   b. MARITAL STATUS
   c. STUDENT LETTER GRADE
   d. UNION MEMBER?   7. _____

8. Which expression best describes the physical view?
   a. a method of proofreading a record
   b. the arrangement of data in a database
   c. a field that can contain TRUE or FALSE or YES or NO
   d. the method in which users view information in the database   8. ____

9. A customer file, containing names and addresses, might also have a field in which users can annotate records when necessary. This field is a
   a. memo field
   b. field name
   c. logical field
   d. source document   9. ____

10. Which information would not be included in documentation for a student database file?
    a. primary and secondary keys
    b. the names of all the students
    c. type and length of all fields
    d. instructions for using the file   10. ____

CHAPTER 3: LOCATING RECORDS AND UPDATING THE FILE

In Chapter 3 you will:

- Determine procedures for locating records.
- Consider the use of search criteria.
- See how new records are added to the file.
- Identify precautions to be taken when deleting records.
- Assess procedures for changing existing records.

Once your database file has been created, much of your time working with it will be spent (1) locating records and (2) updating the file. When updating the file, you will change, add, and delete records to keep the file current.

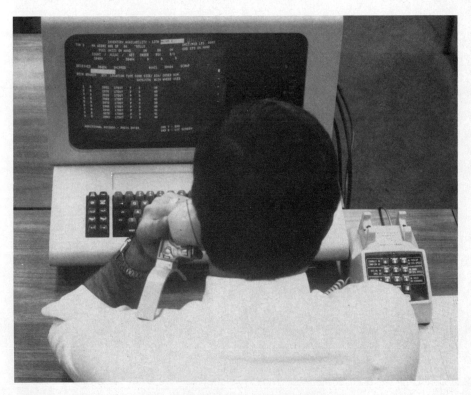

A DBMS can provide its users with information within seconds.

LOCATING RECORDS

One of the most important uses of a DBMS is to allow you to quickly locate information in the file. For example, a sales representative who fills orders by telephone may use a database to find information in seconds while he or she is on the telephone.

The sales representative, Martin Bollinger, receives a phone call from a customer requesting that certain items be shipped as soon as possible. He immediately searches the customer database file for that customer's credit rating to see if shipment can be made prior to payment. Next, the inventory database is searched to determine whether all ordered items are in stock. If an item is not in stock, Bollinger tells the customer when to expect shipment. Having to wait until a shipment is received to find out that some of the items are out of stock is very annoying. Knowing immediately which items are in stock gives the customer a feeling of confidence in Bollinger and his company.

```
LIST FOR CNAME =

      CUSTNO = 29541
```

The salesperson searches the database for customer number 29541.

Note that E is the coded field for Excellent. →

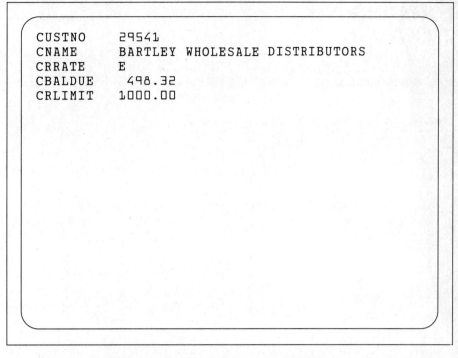

```
CUSTNO      29541
CNAME       BARTLEY WHOLESALE DISTRIBUTORS
CRRATE      E
CBALDUE      498.32
CRLIMIT     1000.00
```

The salesperson now knows that this customer's credit rating is excellent and that shipment can be made prior to payment.

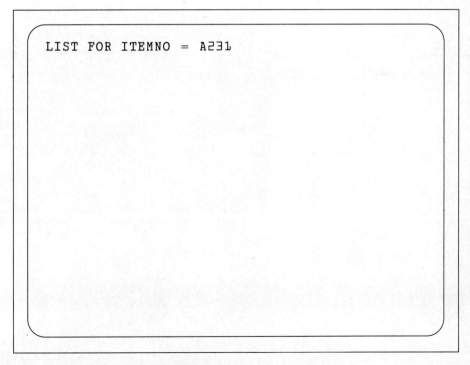

```
LIST FOR ITEMNO = A231
```

The salesperson next searches the database for item number A231.

Note that there are 20 Model 8-A telephones in stock. →

```
ITEMNO      A231
DESCR       MODEL 8-A TELEPHONE
PRICE       39.99
QTYONHND    20
REORDRPT    50
ONORDER     50
SHPDATE     1104
```

If the customer does not want more than 20 Model 8-A telephones, the order can be filled now. If more than 20 are requested, the salesperson can say that the item can be shipped on November 4 (1104), when the company will have another 50 Model 8-A telephones in stock.

With a DBMS, this pharmacist can quickly determine if a perscription can be refilled.

The speed with which you can provide answers to questions is one of the most powerful features of a DBMS. Let's look at other situations in which a DBMS can be of great value.

- A pharmacist searches a prescription file to tell a customer whether or not a prescription can be refilled.
- A purchasing agent finds the name of the vendor from whom the company purchases parts which are urgently needed by the maintenance crew.
- To prepare for annual salary reviews, a personnel manager determines which employees were hired in the current month.
- A lawyer locates the address of the insurance company which is liable for damages in a client's lawsuit.
- A sales manager finds which sales representatives have sales of more than $25,000 for the month.
- A customer relations manager determines which customers in Detroit have account balances over $5,000 or have been customers for more than 5 years.
- A salesperson obtains a listing of all customers not contacted since last month.

When looking for a record, you can do a *sequential record search*, which means starting your search with the first record and looking at each one until you reach the last record. A sequential search is fine when you are looking for the same information in every record. For most searches, however, it is much faster to enter search criteria and allow the DBMS to find the records which match the criteria.

Search criteria are facts about the records you want to find. For example, when a salesperson taking telephone orders is told the customer's name or number, only that name or number is keyed into the computer to locate the record. The database program will immediately find and display the customer's account on the computer screen.

Some DBMSs are *command-driven*, which means that you must key a search command such as LIST, FIND, or DISPLAY CUSTOMER NAME = (name). Suppose you want to retrieve information about Hector J. Sommers. The DBMS you are using has a "dot prompt" on the computer screen, which is a signal to you that the software is ready for a command. Notice the search command in the illustration on page 34.

```
DISPLAY FOR NAME = SOMMERS HECTOR J
```

Command-driven database.

```
1. DESIGN FILE          4. DELETE

2. ADD A RECORD         5. PRINT

3. SEARCH/UPDATE        6. EXIT

   SELECTION NUMBER:  3

   FILE NAME:
```

Menu-driven database. The selection screen allows you to choose the option you desire.

```
CUSTNO

CUSTNAME    SOMMERS HECTOR J

CADDRESS

CITY                               STATE        ZIP

CRRATNG                  CRLIMIT            BALDUE
```

To find Hector J. Sommers' record, move the cursor to the CUSTNAME field and key his name. All records with SOMMERS HECTOR J will be retrieved. This menu-driven database was adapted from PFS File.

Other databases are *menu-driven*, which means they allow you to select the search option from a list of choices called a menu. After you have selected the search option, the record layout will appear on the screen. When this happens, move the cursor to CUSTNAME, key the customer's name, and press the enter or return key. All records having the keyed name will be retrieved.

Searches are often executed using the primary key, such as the customer number. (A primary key, as you will recall from Chapter 2, is the key field that is consulted first when retrieving records.) When the primary key is used, your DBMS should retrieve just one record because each record has a different primary key. If you use a secondary key, it is possible that your DBMS will retrieve several records. When several records are retrieved, you can browse through each record. To *browse*, you move the cursor downward through the selected records, displaying one record at a time.

When specifying your search criteria, you may specify the logic of your search using a *relational operator*. Several relational, or logical, operators are listed here:

Relational Operators

> Greater than
< Less than
= Equal to
>= Greater than or equal to
<= Less than or equal to
<> Not equal to

AND and OR are used when more than one search criterion must be specified.

You would use a relational operator if, for example, you wanted to search for all customers whose account balance is greater than $5,000. If in your search you specify the following:

```
CUSTBAL > 5000
```

these records will be retrieved:

Customer Name	Balance
ELONZO WELLS	6000.00
JONATHAN ELLINGTON	6500.00
MARGUERITE WHEATLEY	7200.00
MARIA GONZALES	5200.00
ANGELINE JEFFERSON	6900.00

Often your search for records will have more than one criterion. Suppose, for example, that you are searching for all customers whose account balance is more than $5,000 or whose credit rating is coded E, for excellent. Because the search has more than one criterion, it is said to have *multiple search criteria*.

If in your search you specify the following:

```
CUSTBAL > 5000 OR CRRATE = E
```

these records will be retrieved:

Customer Name	Credit Rating	Balance
JEFF PARKER	E	1000.00
ELONZO WELLS	E	6000.00
JONATHAN ELLINGTON	G	6500.00
MARGUERITE WHEATLEY	P	7200.00
MARIA GONZALES	E	5200.00
ANTONIO LANDES	E	3300.00
ANGELINE JEFFERSON	G	6900.00

Note that every record meets the condition of having a balance greater than $5,000 or a credit rating of E.

When using multiple search criteria, either the connector OR or the connector AND is used. In the example above, OR was used. Records were retrieved that matched *either* condition. However, when you use AND in your search statement, a record must match *both* conditions in order to be retrieved. If the above example were changed to read:

```
CUSTBAL > 5000 AND CRRATE = E
```

only the following records will be retrieved:

Customer Name	Credit Rating	Balance
ELONZO WELLS	E	6000.00
MARIA GONZALES	E	5200.00

PARTIAL MATCH SEARCHES

Sometimes when you search for a record, you may know only part of the contents of a field. For example, you want to phone a vendor named Stevens, but you don't recall the first name. One way to retrieve the record is to specify VENDOR NAME = STEVENS and browse through the file until you recognize the correct Stevens. Another procedure that can be used with most DBMSs is to specify only the first or last few characters of the search criteria. With some DBMSs it is possible to search for records in which the search field contains certain characters located anywhere within the field. For example, when you key . . SMITH . . using PFS File, the following records in a database will be retrieved:

```
SMITH JACK C
PERRY SMITHSON J
SMITHERS CECILIA ANN
SILVERSMITH CARRIE
KNOX MARY SMITH
```

THE WILD-CARD SEARCH

In many card games, certain cards are said to be "wild" when they can be used to take the place of any card in the deck. Similarly, a *wild card* in a computer search is a character that can be used to take the place of any character in the file. Most DBMSs permit you to search for information when the field contents are only partially known, as in the example above. These searches are done by keying one or more wild-card characters along with the limited information that is known. Depending upon the database software you are using, the wild-card character may be the asterisk (*), two periods (. .), the *at* symbol (@), the question mark (?), and certain other characters. For example, suppose you want to search for a customer's record but you aren't sure if the customer's name is Chris Kelly or Chris Kelsy. You could use the wild-card search by keying KEL**. The following records would be retrieved:

```
KELLY LISA
KELLY THOMAS
KELSY CHRIS
```

UPDATING THE FILE

A database file requires frequent maintenance. New records are added, inactive records are deleted, and existing records are changed. The process of adding, deleting, and changing is called *updating* the file.

ADDING RECORDS

With most DBMSs, when you add a new record, you actually *append* (add) the new record onto the end of the file. When you give the appropriate add command, your screen will display prompts or field names. You then key the data for the new record, proofread it, and press enter or return. Some DBMSs will assign a number to the record, and the number will appear on the screen as the last number in the sequence of records in the file.

A few DBMSs will allow you to *insert* a record into the file between two existing records. For example, you can insert a record between record 16 and record 17. In this case, old record 17 becomes record 18, and the new one becomes record 17.

DELETING RECORDS

Great care must be taken when deleting records. Once a record has been removed from your file, you may not be able to recover it. Double-check to ensure that the record you tell the computer to delete has the correct key field so that you don't accidentally delete a record you had intended to keep. Most DBMS software will display a question on the screen asking you to verify (yes or no) that you wish to delete a record. This gives you a chance to change your mind.

Some DBMSs allow you to recover deleted records if they have been deleted logically but not physically. In this case, when you first issue the command to delete a record, it is *logically deleted* (marked for deletion) rather than physically deleted. This means that the record is still on your data disk but the software has placed a mark by it to indicate it is no longer to be treated as if it exists. It is not *physically deleted* until you issue another command to cause the record to be actually removed from the diskette and all other records to be moved up to take its place. Software with this capability, often called the *undelete* feature, allows you to recover the record before you have physically removed it from the file.

Most database software does not allow such recovery, so be very cautious when deleting. If you make a mistake and delete the wrong record, the only way to recover it will be to key it again as a new record. It is wise to have a hard copy of the record before deleting it, in case you wish to key it into your file again.

CHANGING RECORDS

When you change a phone number, an address, or a pay rate, the file is being updated. You do this by issuing the command to change a record. The DBMS first asks you to enter the key field or some other search criterion to locate the record that is to be changed.

Once your record has been retrieved, you simply move the cursor to the field or fields to be changed and key the new data, which take the place of the old.

When updating records, you should again be very cautious. Once you have keyed a change, there is usually no way to recover the old data in the field. It is therefore wise to keep a hard copy of your old records before any new changes are made.

VOCABULARY

append	physical deletion
browse	relational operator
command-driven	search criteria
insert	sequential record search
logical deletion	undelete
menu-driven	update
multiple search criteria	wild card

CHAPTER 3
SELF-CHECK REVIEW

TRUE OR FALSE

Identify each of the following statements as true or false by circling T or F. Check your answers on page 101 when you have finished.

1. One of the most valuable features of a DBMS is the speed with which you can locate records.   T   F

2. A sequential record search will search a file from beginning to end.   T   F

3. Search criteria are specified facts a record must have in order for it to be retrieved.   T   F

4. If a search criterion is the primary key, several records should be retrieved.   T   F

5. If a search criterion is a secondary key, only one record can be retrieved.   T   F

6. A command-driven DBMS allows the user to select options from a menu to execute searches.   T   F

7. In using multiple search criteria with the AND connector, a record must match both conditions in order to be retrieved.   T   F

8. A wild-card search locates records in which a portion of a field is not known.   T   F

9. A relational operator is also known as a wild card.   T   F

10. A logically deleted record can never be recovered.   T   F

11. After changes to records have been completed, the original information can be recovered if needed.   T   F

12. It is wise to have a hard copy of records before they are updated.   T   F

13. A physically deleted record can be recovered.   T   F

14. If a new record is inserted between record 23 and record 24, the new record becomes record 24.   T   F

MULTIPLE CHOICE

For each statement, select the best choice and write the letter of your choice in the blank. Check your answers on page 102 when you have finished.

1. Starting a search with the first record and look-ing at each one until you reach the last record is called a
    a. criterion search
    b. sequential search
    c. relational search
    d. wild-card search   1. ____

2. Database software that allows you to select op-tions from a list of choices on the screen is said to be
    a. relational
    b. operator-driven
    c. command-driven
    d. menu-driven   2. ____

3. To retrieve one specific record in which all the field contents are known, your search criterion should first use the
    a. primary key
    b. wild card
    c. relational operator
    d. secondary key   3. ____

4. To __?__ is to move the cursor downward through each of several retrieved records.
    a. update
    b. delete
    c. browse
    d. append   4. ____

5. Which relational operator will cause retrieval of records for all customers whose balance is less than \$1,000 as well as for all customers whose credit rating is poor?
    a. CUSTBAL > 1000 AND CRRATE = P
    b. CUSTBAL < 1000 OR CRRATE = P
    c. CUSTBAL < 1000 AND CRRATE = P
    d. CUSTBAL < 1000 AND CRRATE + P   5. ____

6. Which relational operator will cause retrieval of records for all customers whose balance is more than $2,000 and who have an excellent credit rating?
   a. CUSTBAL > 2000 OR CRRATE = E
   b. CUSTBAL < 2000 OR CRRATE = E
   c. CUSTBAL < 2000 AND CRRATE = E
   d. CUSTBAL > 2000 AND CRRATE = E   6. ____

7. Which name will be retrieved if .. is a wild-card format and the search criterion is ..well.. ?
   a. Welcome Wagon, Inc.
   b. Andrew W. Ellerson, Attorney
   c. Geneva D. Stillwell, MD
   d. Bell Taco House   7. ____

8. Updating a file includes which activities?
   a. add, change, delete
   b. design, input, search
   c. physically and logically delete
   d. browse, append, insert   8. ____

9. Database software having the undelete feature can mark a record for deletion without
   a. using a relational operator
   b. physically deleting the record
   c. logically deleting the record
   d. performing a sequential search   9. ____

10. It is wise to have __?__ of records before deleting them from the database file.
   a. summaries
   b. filenames
   c. wild cards
   d. hard copies   10. ____

SHORT ANSWER

Complete each statement by writing the missing word or words in the blank spaces on the right. Check your answers on page 102 when you have finished.

1. __?__ are facts a record must match in order for it to be located and retrieved.   1. _____

2. Greater than (>), less than (<), equal to (=), greater than or equal to (>=), less than or equal to (<=), and not equal to (<>) are examples of __?__.   2. _____

3. If a search has more than one criterion, you are using __?__ search criteria.

3. _____

4. A partial match or __?__ search is used when some of the contents of a field are not known.

4. _____

5. Adding records to an existing file may be referred to as __?__ the file.

5. _____

6. A __?__ deleted record is one that has been marked for removal but can still be recovered.

6. _____

7. A __?__ deleted record is one that has been removed from the file and cannot be recovered.

7. _____

8. A __?__ __?__ DBMS allows a user to choose options from a list on the screen to create and maintain a database file.

8. _____

9. Software with the __?__ capability permits recovery of a record before physical deletion takes place.

9. _____

10. To __?__ through records, move the cursor downward through selected records so that the records are displayed one at a time.

10. _____

USING RELATIONAL OPERATORS

For each of the following search criteria, which records from the file below will be retrieved? Write the letter of each record in the space beside the search criteria. Some letters can be used more than once, and some answers involve more than one letter. A record can be the correct answer to more than one question. If no records would be retrieved, write *none* in the blank. Check your answers on page 102 when you have finished.

1. AGE <= 35 AND SEX = F   1. _____
2. YRSSERV > 25 OR AGE > 60   2. _____
3. TYPE = W AND RATE < 10.00   3. _____
4. SEX = F AND TYPE = B   4. _____
5. TYPE = W AND DEPT =
    PROD   5. _____
6. DEPT = ACCT AND SEX = M   6. _____
7. DEPT = ACCT OR TYPE = B   7. _____

	SS#	EMPLOYEE	AGE	SEX	YRSSERV	RATE	TYPE	DEPT
a.	344-87-8892	Jane Burton	25	F	6	7.95	W	Prod
b.	576-28-7611	Renaldo Degas	38	M	16	12.92	W	Ship
c.	220-77-0034	Cecilia Young	42	F	20	2225.18	B	Acct
d.	231-06-8722	Joe Goldberg	53	M	23	2415.04	B	Prod
e.	472-53-2845	May O'Brian	62	F	24	15.67	W	Prod
f.	144-09-9643	Jean Yen	65	F	18	2029.85	B	Asmb
g.	552-78-4738	Earl Cole	58	M	30	2996.74	W	Asmb

Note: The field YRSSERV contains the number of years served by each employee. The coded field TYPE indicates whether the employee is paid weekly (W) or biweekly (B).

CHAPTER 4: SORTING, LISTING, AND REPORTING

In Chapter 4 you will:

- Identify procedures for sorting records alphabetically and numerically.
- Distinguish between ascending and descending sorts.
- Identify primary and secondary key sorts.
- Recognize case sensitivity in databases.
- Distinguish between listings and reports.
- Determine how listings and reports are produced.
- Review documentation techniques.

SORTING RECORDS

In the first three chapters of this book, you examined the process of creating a database file and entering, updating, and accessing records. This chapter deals with producing printed output, or hard copy, from a database file. One of the outstanding features of database software is its efficiency in sorting, listing, and reporting information.

Reports may be timely and accurate, but they will be of little value unless the information is arranged in a logical sequence. Therefore, records are usually sorted before being printed. *Sorted records* are records in a certain sequence or order. A file can be sorted either alphabetically or numerically by a chosen field. The order of sorting may be *ascending* (a–z, 0–9) or *descending* (z–a, 9–0) for both alphabetic and numeric sorting.

The screens on pages 46 and 47 illustrate sorted records.

Sometimes it is necessary to sort records by more than one field in the same listing. For example, you may want to list employees alphabetically by department. In such a list, the department names are arranged alphabetically and the employees in each department are listed alphabetically within each department. The department represents the *major* or *primary sort key*. The employee names within each department are also alphabetized. Therefore, their names constitute the *minor* or *secondary sort key*.

Many DBMSs allow more than two sort keys or fields. Consult your software reference manual to find the maximum number of fields that can be sorted at one time.

Some software generates a separate sorted file each time a sort command is executed. The original unsorted file is not disturbed.

```
NAME                    EMP NO   DEPT

ANDREWS  BARBARA        A113     SHIPPING
COLLINS  DONALD         C226     ACCOUNTING
COLLINS  JOHN           C228     PURCHASING
EDWARDS  JOSEPH         E667     PURCHASING
FENDERSON  JOAN         F412     ACCOUNTING
HILL  DOUGLAS           H338     SHIPPING
MCMICHAEL  MARTIN       M770     ACCOUNTING
ORITZ  MIGUEL           O361     SALES
POPEK  LEON             P894     ACCOUNTING
VANHORN  COLLEEN        V769     SALES
```

An employee listing sorted alphabetically by the NAME field in ascending order.

```
                ITEM
PRICE           CODE    ITEM NAME                   SERIAL NO

   150.00       PR01    CHECK PROTECTOR             P66849
   295.00       AM01    ANSWERING MACHINE           M099437C
   485.00       DM01    DICTATING MACHINE           99870600
   680.00       TY01    ELECTRONIC TYPEWRITER       4886A43
   799.00       TY04    ELECTRONIC TYPEWRITER       0033340E
  1200.00       CP11    COMPUTER TERMINAL           T7768436
  3995.00       CP04    PRINTER                     L69430A
  7100.00       CP03    PRINTER                     M665782
 17225.00       CP04    COMPUTER SYSTEM             PCC8476A
```

An inventory listing sorted numerically by the PRICE field in ascending order.

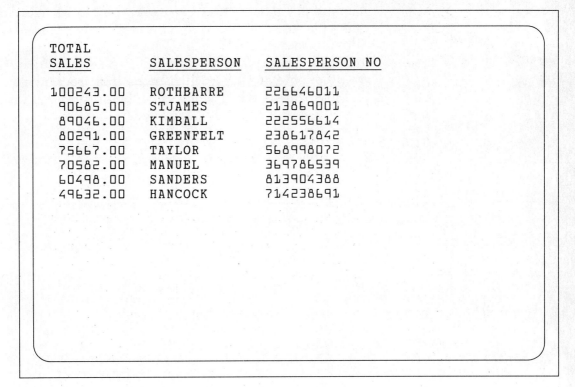

```
TOTAL
SALES            SALESPERSON       SALESPERSON NO

 100243.00       ROTHBARRE         226646011
  90685.00       STJAMES           213869001
  89046.00       KIMBALL           222556614
  80291.00       GREENFELT         238617842
  75667.00       TAYLOR            568998072
  70582.00       MANUEL            369786539
  60498.00       SANDERS           813904388
  49632.00       HANCOCK           714238691
```

A real estate sales listing sorted numerically by the TOTAL SALES field in descending order.

```
DEPT             NAME                  DOB        POSITION

ACCOUNTING       ALLEN JOEL P          08/29/48   CLERK
ACCOUNTING       BEZZINI MARIO S       07/15/65   ACCTS PAY
ACCOUNTING       FULLER JAMES P        01/14/50   ACCOUNTANT
MARKETING        FUJITA SUMIO          12/16/49   RESEARCH
MARKETING        POPEK LEON W          10/31/61   REPRESENTATIVE
PRODUCTION       ALSAQE ROBERT F       05/16/52   QUALITY CONTROL
PRODUCTION       HALSTROM RK           07/08/66   MANAGER
PRODUCTION       KIM CHEE WON          11/10/61   LINE WORKER
PRODUCTION       STJAMES SANDRA T      06/08/59   LINE WORKER
SHIPPING         HILLDOWNING AJ        05/11/49   MANAGER
SHIPPING         KIMBELL CYNTHIA C     06/06/56   CLERK
SHIPPING         SHELLEY D SANDERS     03/06/59   DRIVER
```

An employee listing sorted primarily by the DEPARTMENT field with the employee name sorted within department. The DEPARTMENT field is the primary key, and the NAME field is the secondary key.

Therefore, after the sort has been completed, you have a second file with the same records, but the records in the new file are in a different order. The two files have separate filenames. After updating records in the original file, you should update and re-sort your new file so that it will also be in correct order.

Other DBMSs simply rearrange the original file into a new order when a sort command is executed.

```
NAME                    RATE

ORITZ RICARDO E          7.50
HILL DOUGLAS J           8.32
MCMICHAEL MARTIN G       6.95
VANHORN COLLEEN T        7.10
CARRERA ADOLFO G        10.80
BARNES ALLEN G           5.65
NIMMO CURTIS B          15.60
HANCE GERALD E           8.90
```

```
NAME                    RATE

BARNES ALLEN G           5.65
CARRERA ADOLFO G        10.80
HANCE GERALD E           8.90
HILL DOUGLAS J           8.32
MCMICHAEL MARTIN G       6.95
NIMMO CURTIS B          15.60
ORITZ RICARDO E          7.50
VANHORN COLLEEN T        7.10
```

The screen on the left is the original unsorted file; the original file name is PAYFLE. The screen on the right is the newly created sorted file; the new filename is SPAYFLE1. This illustration is specific to dBase software by Ashton Tate.

THE ASCII CODE AND CASE SENSITIVITY

Records are sorted by a coding scheme—usually the ASCII code discussed on page 24. Each character is assigned a number for sorting purposes.

Because the ASCII code sorts characters by the assigned number value, punctuation and symbols come before numbers, numbers come before uppercase letters, and uppercase letters come before lowercase letters. Within the ASCII code, like characters are sorted together. Therefore, to ensure that the database will sort properly, the data in each record in a file must exist in the same case, either upper or lower. If names of individuals are to be sorted extensively, the names should be entered in all uppercase letters. Note the problem that can occur if this is not done:

Names as Entered	*Names Sorted by ASCII Code*
Deemer	DeLong
DeLong	Deemer

DeLong is sorted before Deemer because ASCII assigns a lower number value to the uppercase letter *L* than to the lowercase letter *e*. Therefore, for correct sorting in a computer database file it is wise to enter names of individuals in all uppercase letters (DEEMER, DELONG). All computers using the ASCII code respond to *case sensitivity*, which is the ability to recognize the distinction between uppercase and lowercase letters.

REPORT VERSUS LISTING

A *report* is a hard-copy list of records in a specific format, and it is formal rather than informal in style. A report may contain:

1. Titles.
2. Columnar titles.
3. Calculated fields and columns.
4. Subtotals.
5. Totals.
6. Counts of records.

The format of a report should be carefully planned for spacing and order. The report may be single-, double-, or triple-spaced. The fields included in a report can be arranged in whatever order the user requires. Titles enhance a report, making the information more understandable.

With many DBMS packages, it is possible to create new fields by performing a calculation using one or more numeric fields from the file. For example, if the wholesale price of an item is stored in the database, it is possible to report the retail price by multiplying the wholesale price by a markup factor. To illustrate, if wholesale price = $50.00 and markup factor = 25 percent, then retail price = $50.00 $\times$ 1.25, or $62.50.

Having subtotals and totals printed is very important to users of reports. For example, if records for a sales report are sorted by store (secondary sort key) within a region (primary sort key), then it would be pertinent to print subtotals of sales figures for each store with a total for each region and a grand total of all sales.

Counts of records are used to show the number of records reported. In a payroll journal, the user may wish to have a count of employees reported within a department and a count of all employees paid by the organization.

Reports are classified into three general types: *detail*, *summary*, and *exception*. Each type has a different purpose.

Type of Report	Content
Detail	Lists every record in the file. This type of report is most often used by the employees of an organization who work daily with the details of the business.
Summary	Lists only subtotals and totals. The summary report is often the only type of report that management wants. Summary information is also of value to the day-to-day workers.
Exception	Lists only the records that meet a specified condition. Both management and other employees often require reports containing information about selected records.

```
                         CLIENT BY TYPE


                                              NUMBER OF
      ACCOUNT     NAME                         SUBSCRIBERS     TYPE


         90      2001 TECHNOLOGIES INC            650           M
        283      RT STANLEY MANUFACTURERS        2500           M
        465      SHORES BAKERY INC                245           M
         66      SILVERTON ELECTRONICS            350           M
        304      SILVERTRON MINING CO             900           M
        600      STOCKTON DAIRIES                 320           M
        242      THURSTON ENTERPRISES            2780           M
        112      VAN TECH INC                    2500           M
        560      VERONA LUMBER CO                 145           M
        420      WB WALKER AND SONS INC           530           M
        180      WAKE CO MANUFACTURING            599           M

    ** SUBTOTAL **                             11519  *

        183      TARGET MS                        780           N
        166      TRUST HELP LINE                   15           N
         95      VARNER RESEARCH CENTER           250           N
        180      WAR AGAINST CANCER               345           N

    ** SUBTOTAL **                              1390  *
```

```
          SUBSCRIBERS BY TYPE

ACCOUNT TYPE      NUMBER OF SUBSCRIBERS


GOVERNMENT              2715
MANUFACTURING          11519
NONPROFIT               1390
RETAIL                 15689
SERVICE                18230
WHOLESALE               7646

   TOTAL               57189 *
```

```
       CLIENTS WITH FEWER THAN 500 SUBSCRIBERS

                               NUMBER OF
ACCOUNT     NAME               SUBSCRIBERS    TYPE

  465     SHORES BAKERY INC         245        M
   66     SILVERTON ELECTRONICS     350        M
  600     STOCKTON DAIRIES          320        M
  560     VERONA LUMBER CO          145        M

** SUBTOTAL **                     1060 *

  166     TRUST HELP LINE            15        N
   95     VARNER RESEARCH CENTER    250        N
  180     WAR AGAINST CANCER        345        N

** SUBTOTAL **                      610 *
```

The example on the left is a page of a *detail report* showing clients sorted alphabetically within organization type. At the end of the report there may be a grand total of all types. The example at the top is a *summary report* providing only the totals for each group and a grand total of all groups. The example at the bottom is an *exception report* showing only those clients having fewer than 500 subscribers.

When it is important to obtain a copy of records in a short amount of time, a listing can be produced. A *listing* is an informal list of records and usually contains column headings and columns of data. Listings do not have formal titles or a special format.

For updating purposes or quick review, a listing can be produced on the screen rather than on paper. This saves both time and resources but does not produce a hard copy of the records. When a paper copy is needed, a hard-copy listing is printed.

The advantage of a listing is that it can be produced quickly. Listings do not necessitate the careful planning required for producing a report.

```
NAME                              ADDRESS                   CITY

SHELTON WILLIAM EDWARD            2425 WOOD LAKE TERRACE     LOUISVILLE
VANHORN COLLEEN T                 2708 FOX HUNT DRIVE        LOUISVILLE
ALSHAMMARI FALEH MOHAMMED         4526 LAUREN CIRCLE         LOUISVILLE
GREENSFELT STEVEN M               2458 BARCA DRIVE           CINCINNATI
MCMICHAEL MARTIN G                RT 6 BOX 6                 REILY
HANCOCK PETER M                   RR 624                     BENNINGTON
SANDERS JERON P                   33 ROCKLAND BOULEVARD      JOPLIN
POPEK LEON W                      654 CLEARWATER COURT       COLUMBUS
KIM CHEE WON                      254 NORTH 25TH STREET      DAYTON
BUSCHMATTOX AMY LEWIS             85 GLOUSTER CIRCLE         LOUISVILLE
ORTIZ EDWARDO RICARDO MIGUEL      2425 LAS MARINAS AVENUE    LOUISVILLE
ORITZ MERCEDES JOAQUINA           656 CABO BLANCO WAY        CINCINNATI
ROZENTHALL THOMAS T               8525 BREEZY LANE           CINCINNATI
HILLDOWNING A                     425 BELMONT AVENUE         CINCINNATI
SAVAGE ERIN P                     1516 ST GEORGE AVENUE      FORT WAYNE
ALSAKE LOU M                      2456 WILLOR ROAD           DAYTON
LIEBMAN ISAAC A                   296 WEDGEWORTH LANE        DAYTON
```

This is a simple listing showing the NAME, ADDRESS, and CITY fields. Notice the listing is informal—no main title, date, or page number. Also, the names are not sorted alphabetically.

REPORT PLAN-NING AND DOCUMENTATION

Many types of reports are run frequently, some are run periodically, and some as needed. For example, most companies produce a payroll journal for each pay period; sales reports are produced daily, weekly, monthly, or quarterly; and reports listing customers with overdue balances may be produced as needed. Each type of report is always in the same format.

The careful planning of a report ensures its usefulness. The layout of a report should be recorded for future reference. Using a report documentation form, such as the one illustrated on the next page, helps ensure that facts about the report are available should changes be made in the future.

REPORT DOCUMENTATION

Title of Report: _____
                                      (line 1)

                          _____
                                      (line 2)

                          _____
                                      (line 3)

Creator(s): _____   Date of Creation:

             _____   ____/____/____
                                                                 mo   day   yr

File From Which Report Is Made: _____

Fields (in order) to Appear in the Report:

1. _____	11. _____
2. _____	12. _____
3. _____	13. _____
4. _____	14. _____
5. _____	15. _____
6. _____	16. _____
7. _____	17. _____
8. _____	18. _____
9. _____	19. _____
10. _____	20. _____

Subtotals (Fields): _____

                         _____

Totals (Fields):   _____

                         _____

Spacing:

Single   _____

Double   _____

Triple   _____

Attach related source document.

The date of creation and names of the creators are recorded in case someone has a question about the report. The file from which the records are taken are noted as well. Good documentation of a report format includes this notation as well as the names of the fields which are used in the report. If subtotals and totals are taken, this fact should be included in the documentation. Any calculated fields, as well as line spacing, should be noted.

Documentation is important to the designer as well as the user of a database file. Reports have many details that may be forgotten in time; therefore, the details of a report should not be committed to memory but should be thoroughly documented.

VOCABULARY

ascending sort   primary sort key
case sensitivity   report
descending sort   secondary sort key
detail report   sorted records
exception report   summary report
listing

CHAPTER 4
SELF-CHECK REVIEW

TRUE OR FALSE

Identify each statement as true or false by circling T or F. Check your answers on page 102 when you have finished.

1. An inventory of spare parts could be sorted into numeric order by part number or alphabetic order by description.   **T**   **F**

2. Numeric fields in a file can be sorted in either ascending or descending order, whereas alphabetic fields are sorted only in ascending order.   **T**   **F**

3. When sorting a parts file by description within warehouse location, the description field is the primary sort key and the warehouse location field is the secondary sort key.   **T**   **F**

4. Some database software creates a separate sorted file without disturbing the original unsorted file.   **T**   **F**

5. When a separate sorted file is created, it has the same filename as the original unsorted file.   **T**   **F**

6. When the original unsorted file is updated, the separate sorted file will also be updated automatically.   **T**   **F**

7. Mixing uppercase and lowercase characters in the same field can cause sorting problems.   **T**   **F**

8. Listings are formal; reports are informal.   **T**   **F**

9. When you want to quickly review records, a listing can be produced on the computer screen.   **T**   **F**

10. Case sensitivity means that the format of a report has been fully documented.   **T**   **F**

11. Spreadsheet software, rather than database software, must be used in preparing reports having subtotals and totals.   **T**   **F**

12. With many DBMS packages, it is possible to create new fields by performing a calculation using one or more numeric fields from the file.   **T**   **F**

MULTIPLE CHOICE

For each statement, select the best choice and write the letter of your choice in the blank. Check your answers on page 102 when you have finished.

1. An example of numbers sorted into ascending order by a numeric sort key is
    a. 245, 248, 323, 284
    b. 245, 248, 284, 285
    c. 323, 284, 245, 248
    d. 323, 284, 248, 245   1. _____

2. Which name will appear first in a list sorted in ascending order using the ASCII code?
    a. DeCorte, Maria
    b. Deavers, Michael
    c. Debusk, Carrie
    d. DeBusk, Donald   2. _____

3. Which name will appear first in a list sorted in descending order?
    a. ABRAMS CONRAD C
    b. YABLONSKI DAVID
    c. WOLF MARIE
    d. PARKINTON FRANCIS   3. _____

4. Which name will appear first in a list sorted in ascending order using the ASCII code?
    a. OBRIAN CARMEN
    b. OAKES KENNETH
    c. OBENCHAIN JOHN
    d. OBRAINE PATRICIA   4. _____

5. A listing usually contains which of the following?
    a. titles, columnar titles, subtotals, and totals
    b. calculated columns, subtotals, and totals
    c. column headings and columns of data
    d. a count of the number of records printed   5. _____

6. A report, as distinguished from a listing,
    a. is often used for purposes of quick review
    b. is always double-spaced for readability
    c. is usually read from the screen rather than from hard copy
    d. is usually produced as hard copy   6. _____

7. An employee payroll journal showing a line for every employee within an organization is an example of which type of report?
   a. detail
   b. summary
   c. exception
   d. listing   7. ____

8. A printout showing only those employees qualified to operate a special welding iron is an example of which type of report?
   a. detail
   b. summary
   c. exception
   d. listing   8. ____

9. A report that has one line showing the total budgeted expenses for each department and one line showing the unspent balance for each department is an example of which type of report?
   a. detail
   b. summary
   c. exception
   d. listing   9. ____

10. Good documentation of a report is important to the
    a. user of the report
    b. designer of the report
    c. user and designer
    d. software vendor   10. ____

CHAPTER 5: DATABASE INTEGRITY, SECURITY, AND SELECTION

In Chapter 5 you will:

- Assess measures to achieve file integrity.
- Consider the need to prepare backup copies.
- Determine how to protect confidential records.
- Explore possibilities for the use of integrated software.
- Develop procedures for evaluating and selecting database software.

FILE INTEGRITY

Once we become accustomed to the computer's power and usability, we may become complacent about taking precautions to protect our database. We may also forget that a database has considerable monetary value. It may have taken hundreds of hours to enter all of the records. To reenter the records would cost a considerable amount of money in salary. Thus, the database may be worth thousands of dollars. Such valuable data can be destroyed in several ways, and it is important to plan for each possibility. We insure our cars, homes, and other property against fires, floods, theft, and other kinds of loss. It is equally important to protect computer programs and data by taking the "insurance" of special planning and precautions that are discussed here. In addition, much of the information in databases is confidential and must be kept secure. Finally, information in a database must be accurate. Protecting computer information from damage and unauthorized use and ensuring that database information is accurate are referred to as maintaining *file integrity*.

SAVING DATA

When entering data in the microcomputer, it is wise to save your data to a disk approximately every half hour. If you lose power while entering or modifying a large number of records, you will lose everything you had entered into the computer since you last saved your file; the data that have not been saved to a disk will be lost. Saving every half hour means the most you will have to rekey is a half hour's worth of work. At the end of your work session, save the entire file to the original data disk *and* to a backup data disk. Depending upon the amount of data and its value, you might store one of the disks in a fireproof file.

PREPARING BACKUP COPIES

One of the easiest things you can do to protect your database is to make regular backups. A *backup* is a copy of your disk containing data files and programs. You should establish a regular schedule for backing up your important files. How often this should be done depends on how difficult it is to re-create the data if the originals are destroyed. Making a backup takes a little extra time and effort, but you may find that it is time well spent.

Your backup copies should be kept in a different physical location than the originals. Otherwise, if a disaster, such as a fire or flood, can destroy your originals, it will probably also destroy the backup copies. Some companies keep a weekly backup in a location that is several miles from the original files, realizing that hurricanes, floods, tornadoes, and other disasters usually affect a large geographic area.

PROOFREADING

To help ensure the integrity of your files, those responsible for keying data should follow strict rules about proofreading. In this text we have suggested that data be carefully proofread before the enter or return key is pressed. In addition, a hard copy of the data should be carefully examined for errors. While these suggestions do not provide a 100 percent guarantee of data accuracy, they can greatly reduce the likelihood of error or omission. It is suggested that, if possible, a person other than the one who keyed the data proofread the hard copy.

PROTECTING CONFIDENTIAL DATA

With many DBMSs it is possible to protect confidential data against unauthorized access through the use of passwords. A *password* is a secret code or name known only by authorized users. The password must be keyed at the computer before the file can be accessed. With most DBMSs, the password is keyed but does not appear on the screen. This prevents someone from looking over your shoulder at the screen to gain unauthorized access to a password.

Users who are authorized to gain access to a file can be granted various levels of access: read-only privileges, the ability to add new records, the ability to change records, or the ability to delete records. With many DBMSs a user can authorize others to have up to his or her level of access. These selective access procedures are achieved through the use of various passwords.

When developing passwords, it is wise to use long words that

```
USERNAME: HOLLINSWORTH
PASSWORD:
* UNAUTHORIZED USAGE - USER FAILURE *

USERNAME: HOLLINSWORTH
PASSWORD:
* UNAUTHORIZED USAGE - USER FAILURE *

USERNAME: HOLLINSWORTH
PASSWORD:
* UNAUTHORIZED USAGE - USER FAILURE *

A >
```

Most software will allow a maximum of three tries before shutting out the unauthorized user.

contain random characters. Using a name of a friend or a commonly used office term may be obvious to someone who tries to break through computer security. Passwords should be changed frequently, and they should be memorized by the users rather than written and kept for reference.

Disks should be kept in a locked storage cabinet or closet. If data are on a hard disk, the computer should be locked in a secure place. Computer locks are available to prevent unauthorized persons from turning the computer on.

HARDWARE AND SOFTWARE MAINTENANCE

It is vital that you establish a regular preventive maintenance schedule for computer hardware. The keyboard should be vacuumed and the disk drive heads cleaned often. Disks must be protected against extreme heat and cold, sunlight, spillage of food or liquids, cigarette smoke, magnets and magnetic fields, and fingerprints.

INTEGRATED SOFTWARE

Frequently you will want to include a spreadsheet or graph in a report or combine the information retrieved from a database with the formula-based information in a spreadsheet. You might want to include a long narrative for documentation in one of your spreadsheet models. There may be times when you would like to combine the ability of a database to generate raw data with the capability of a word processor to manipulate the data into a finished text. In other words, you may want your software to perform several functions. Software that can perform two or more functions is known as *integrated software*.

Four of the most popular programs found in integrated software packages are the database, word processor, spreadsheet, and graphics programs. The *database* is a collection of related files stored in a computer; use the database to process, access, and retrieve information. The *word processor* is a program that manipulates alphanumeric characters to serve various communication purposes; use the word processor to execute memos, letters, and other documents. The *spreadsheet* is a program based on an accountant's ledger in which figures are presented in columns and rows; use the spreadsheet to perform calculations. The *graphics* software is a program in which information is entered into a computer and displayed on a screen as a graph, chart, table, or other illustration; use graphics software to design illustrations.

Imagine that you work for a wholesaler who distributes magazines, newspapers, books, and videos to the various retail stores in your city. In your database you have information about each retailer that includes the products distributed to that merchant as well as the amounts of sales and the returns for credit. You have

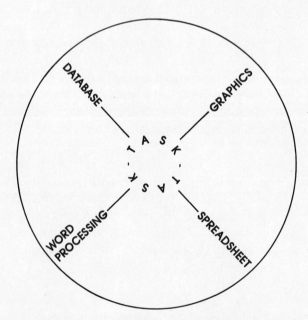

Integrated software allows you to use the best tool available to get the job done. Some things can be done more efficiently and more easily with a database or a spreadsheet; others, with a word processor or graphics.

been asked to prepare a report showing the net dollar sales (sales minus returns for credit) by product type. Using the database, you decide to sort the data by product type. Using the spreadsheet, you obtain the total dollar sales for each type. Using graphics software, you can produce a pie chart showing the sales by product type. You use your word processing software to produce the written part of the report.

Multiple functions such as inventory, cost, and time control programs are available through the use of an integrated software package. Several packages on the market integrate a word processor with spreadsheet, database, graphics, and communication software. Some packages allow integration on accounting func-

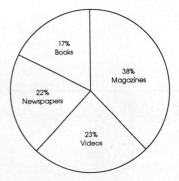

For the month of November, magazines were still the leader with sales of $546,285. Videos are increasing rapidly with a volume of sales of $241,052 in October to $326,191 this month. Newspapers are holding steady at $314,918, and book sales are at $247,775. The chart below illustrates the volume of sales by product type.

17%
Books

38%
Magazines

22%
Newspapers

23%
Videos

In comparing this month's report with last month's, you will notice that magazine sales increased by 6 percent. One probable reason for this is the holiday special editions which always stimulate

With integrated software, the user combined the database, spreadsheet, word processor, and graphics programs to create this report.

tions, in which debits and credits are entered, and manufacturing functions, in which one could control raw materials. For example, by integrating accounting and manufacturing functions, a user could see how costly it is to change a raw material such as iron into steel. It is quite easy to transfer data between functions when using integrated packages. However, some integrated packages tend to be dominated by the base program around which the software is built. They are usually expensive; you have to pay for all of the functions even if you do not need all of them. Integrated packages normally require a great deal of memory, and some may require additional hardware.

An alternative to the integrated package is software that is sold in independent components known as *modules*. An example of this is the PFS series. Each module—word processor, database, spreadsheet—is sold separately. Thus you have to buy only the functions you need, and the functions can easily be combined.

A major advantage to purchasing either integrated or modular software is that the commands and editing features are compatible for all functions. This means that you will have to learn only one set of commands and editing features.

When purchasing software, one can select either a complete integrated software package or the individual programs desired from modular software.

If you use several different independent software packages, it is still possible for you to combine the best features of each of them. Following the directions in your manual, you can change the data from one package into the format needed by another. Most packages allow such transfer if the data are in ASCII form. Others allow transfer only if the data are in DIF (Data Interchange Format) or in SYLK (Symbolic Linkage). Unfortunately, not all packages can be successfully combined. For example, with certain independent software packages, you might be able to include a spreadsheet in a report, but you might not be able to include a graph.

CHOOSING SOFTWARE

Deciding which commercial software packages to buy can be a very difficult task. Hundreds of different packages are available. It takes a great deal of preparation, research, and thought to select the right one.

Before you make a decision, you should make a list of the features you need. Then you should carefully examine each package under consideration and check off the features one by one. You should be allowed to see the software demonstrated and to try it out yourself.

Here is a checklist for the selection of computer software:

1. How *user-friendly* is it? Is it driven by easy-to-use menus? Or is it command-driven?
2. Is it fully *documented*? (Documentation here refers to the printed manuals and brochures that accompany the software.) Is the documentation clear and easy to read? Are directions easy to follow?
3. Is a tutorial provided? (A *tutorial* is an instructional program, usually on disk.) Does the vendor offer classes? Is there a hot line for assistance? (A *hot line* is a telephone number, usually toll-free, which can be called for assistance.) Does the software have a help function? (The *help function* permits you to ask questions about the software while you are using it, and the answers appear on the screen.)
4. Is a template provided? (A *template* is a piece of plastic or cardboard that fits over the function keys on your computer keyboard to label the function of each key.)
5. Do the *hardware requirements* match your computer, or will you have to upgrade memory or add other costly enhancements?
6. Is it *compatible* with other software?
7. Is the software being purchased from a *reputable dealer*?
8. Is the software *recommended* by others?

If you do your homework by using a checklist such as the one here, you are likely to be satisfied with the package you purchase.

CHECKLIST FOR CHOOSING SOFTWARE

Rate the software on each of the following criteria using a 5-point scale where

1 = not available   4 = good
2 = poor   5 = very good or excellent
3 = satisfactory

User-Friendly

_____ Menu-driven.

_____ Command-driven.

_____ Choice of menu- or command-driven.

Documentation

_____ Documentation is easy to read.

_____ Directions are clear, concise, and easy to follow.

Learning

_____ A tutorial is provided.

_____ Vendor offers classes.

_____ Hot line for assistance is provided.

_____ Software has a help function.

Ease of Use

_____ A template is provided.

_____ Function keys used to shorten steps.

Hardware Requirements

_____ My present computer is compatible with the software.
(If not compatible, list below the enhancements required and their costs.)

_____ _____

_____ _____

_____ _____

Other Considerations

_____ Compatibility with other software.

_____ Reputation of the dealer.

_____ Recommended by other users.

_____ Upgrades and enhancements to the software will be provided at a nominal cost.

VOCABULARY

backup   password
file integrity   spreadsheet
graphics   template
help function   tutorial
hot line   user-friendly
integrated software   word processor
modular software

CHAPTER 5
SELF-CHECK REVIEW

TRUE OR FALSE

Identify each statement as true or false by circling T or F. Check your answers on page 102 when you have finished.

1. A database has monetary value.   T   F

2. File integrity refers to the reputation of the software dealer.   T   F

3. It is necessary to make backup copies of software programs only, not data files.   T   F

4. Backup copies of disks should be kept with the originals so they will not become misplaced or lost.   T   F

5. When entering data at the computer, it is wise to save your data to a disk about every half hour.   T   F

6. If you lose power while using a computer, any data on the disks in the drives are erased.   T   F

7. If you lose power while using a computer, any data in the computer's memory are lost.   T   F

8. Because of the editing features of the modern computer, proofreading is no longer necessary.   T   F

9. If possible, a person other than the one who keyed the data should proofread the hard copy.   T   F

10. With most DBMSs, the password is keyed but does not appear on the screen.   T   F

11. Selective access is achieved through the use of various filenames.   T   F

12. When making up passwords, it is wise to use long words which contain random characters.   T   F

13. Software that can perform more than one function is known as integrated software.   T   F

14. Software sold in modules allows the user to purchase only those functions needed.   T   F

15. The ASCII code can be used to transfer data from any software package to any other package.   T   F

MULTIPLE CHOICE

For each statement, select the best choice and write the letter of your choice in the blank. Check your answers on page 103 when you have finished.

1. Which best describes file integrity?
   a. making backup copies of magnetic media every half hour
   b. protection from damage, unauthorized use, and inaccuracy
   c. having a software supplier who can be counted on when assistance is needed
   d. using integrated software to combine the functions of the computer   1. ____

2. Which functions might be combined through the use of integrated software?
   a. database, spreadsheet, and word processing
   b. sorting, retrieving, and accessing
   c. graphics, communications, and proofreading
   d. spreadsheet, printing, and selective access   2. ____

3. Which is an advantage to purchasing software that is sold in modules?
   a. You have a separate disk for each function.
   b. It is easier to use than regular integrated software.
   c. It processes data much faster than regular integrated software.
   d. You have to buy only the functions you need.   3. ____

4. A database package whose program is driven by easy-to-use menus is said to be
   a. integrated
   b. multiple functioned
   c. user-friendly
   d. independent   4. ____

5. The printed manuals and brochures that accompany database software are referred to as
   a. backups
   b. hard copy
   c. documentation
   d. modules   5. ____

6. An instructional program that accompanies software is called
   a. a tutorial
   b. a manual
   c. a module
   d. documentation   6. ____

7. A hot line is
   a. a sudden loss of power
   b. underscored text
   c. an inoperative disk drive
   d. a phone assistance number   7. ____

8. A piece of plastic that fits over the function keys to label each function is a
   a. key label
   b. function marker
   c. password
   d. template   8. ____

9. Graphics software is used to
   a. retrieve data
   b. design illustrations
   c. protect confidential records
   d. perform calculations   9. ____

10. Help functions
    a. prevent unauthorized users from gaining access to confidential data
    b. protect computer information from damage
    c. provide answers to questions users might have about the software
    d. provide 100 percent accuracy   10. ____

DATABASE PROJECT

This database project gives you an opportunity to apply what you have learned in Chapters 1 through 5 of the text. It is adapted from one of the projects in another McGraw-Hill publication written by the authors, *101 Database Exercises*.

HI-TECH FABRICATORS, INVENTORY FILE

The office equipment owned and leased by Hi-Tech Fabricators must be carefully maintained so that time is not lost when the equipment malfunctions. In the past, department managers at Hi-Tech have had difficulty in scheduling office equipment maintenance, repair, and replacement. Records related to items of equipment have not been well organized, and numerous inaccuracies have been detected in the records.

Because of these problems, managers at Hi-Tech have decided to convert the paper recordkeeping system to a computerized database. The managers anticipate that the conversion will lead to much more efficient scheduling of service, repair, and replacement of all office equipment. Additional advantages should also accrue after the equipment inventory has been placed in a computer database. For example, questions about the status of any equipment item or group of items can be answered immediately.

The managers have decided to hire a consultant to convert the old system to a computer database and operate the system for a few days. Because you have completed the chapters in *Quick Guide to Database Management*, the managers have hired *you*. Congratulations!

DESIGNING A FILE

The office supervisor has prepared an Equipment Inventory List of all equipment to be placed in the original computer inventory. Remove page 93, which contains the Equipment Inventory List, so you can look at it as you continue reading. The list has 11 columns as follows:

Item code The office manager has assigned each piece of equipment a unique code which will serve as the key field in this file. Note that each item code has two letters followed by two numbers. The two letters represent the type of equipment, and the two numbers identify the individual machine within that type of equipment. For example, the third (03) computer terminal (CT) has an item code of CT03.

Item name Item name is the type of equipment in inventory.

Department Hi-Tech has three departments: Administration, Sales, and Production.

Date purchased/leased This is the date on which the equipment was originally obtained. The year comes first, followed by the month and the day. Using this date arrangement permits the sorting of items by date.

Purchased/leased Some of the equipment has been purchased (P), and some has been leased (L).

Expiration date This is the month and day on which the annual warranty or service contract on the equipment expires or ends.

Serial number This is the identification code marked on each piece of equipment by the manufacturer.

Cost This is the amount paid for purchased equipment or the value of the leased equipment.

Service vendor This is the business which has been selected to do any service or repair work on the item.

Last service date This is the year, month, and day on which the equipment was last serviced or repaired.

Manufacturer The manufacturer is the company that produced the equipment.

Complete Task 1 as instructed on the next page.

TASK 1
DESIGN THE FILE

Using your database software, design a file for the equipment inventory of Hi-Tech Fabricators. Fill in the blanks below to document your design. Hand in this answer sheet to your instructor. The first field has been filled in as an example.

Field Title	Length	Type
ITEM CODE	4	Alphanumeric
_____	___	_____
_____	___	_____
_____	___	_____
_____	___	_____
_____	___	_____
_____	___	_____
_____	___	_____
_____	___	_____
_____	___	_____

TASK 2
INPUT AND
PROOFREAD
DATA

Using the database file that you designed in Task 1, key in the data for Hi-Tech's equipment inventory from the Equipment Inventory List. Carefully proofread each record after it has been keyed. Then, reading only from your computer screen, answer the following questions about the database. Hand in this answer sheet to your instructor.

1. What is the item name for the machine having item code LP01?

1. _____

2. What is the item code for the equipment manufactured by Scantek?

2. _____

3. Is item CS01 purchased or leased?

3. _____

4. In what department is item ET03 housed?

4. _____

5. What is the expiration date for item FM01?

5. _____

6. Who is the service vendor for item CM01?

6. _____

7. What was the cost of the burster?

7. _____

8. What is the last service date of item PS01?

8. _____

9. What is the date leased of item CT06?

9. _____

10. What is the serial number of item LP01?

10. _____

TASK 3
LIST AND
PROOFREAD
DATA

Sort the file by item code in ascending order. Then print a copy of the file listing all data in every record. Proofread the file again, checking the printout against the original Equipment Inventory List. Then, reading only from your hard copy, answer the following questions about the database. Hand in this answer sheet along with the original Equipment Inventory List to your instructor.

1. Who is the manufacturer of item ET02?

2. What is the item code for the product manufactured by Fonfax?

3. Between which item codes does item CS01 appear?

4. What is the item name for item PS01?

5. Is item CT07 purchased or leased?

6. What is the expiration date for item QP01?

7. Between which item codes does item ET03 appear?

8. What was the last service date of the scanner?

9. In what department is the lap top computer housed?

10. Between which item codes does the laser printer appear?

1. _____

2. _____

3. _____

4. _____

5. _____

6. _____

7. _____

8. _____

9. _____

10. _____

TASK 4
SEARCH FOR
RECORDS

Using your computer database, answer the following questions by performing the appropriate search procedure. Hand in this answer sheet to your instructor.

1. How many items of equipment are serviced by Venus Repair?

1. _____

2. How many items of equipment are serviced by City Computer Repair?

2. _____

3. How many pieces of equipment were purchased or leased before 88/01/01?

3. _____

4. How many pieces of equipment were purchased or leased in 1989?

4. _____

5. On which items will the warranty or service contract expire in June? Report item code, department, and expiration date for each on the lines below.

Item Code	Department	Expiration Date
_____	_____	_____
_____	_____	_____
_____	_____	_____
_____	_____	_____
_____	_____	_____

6. How many pieces of computer equipment (item code beginning with C) are being leased?

6. _____

7. What are the item codes for all machines being maintained by Supra Machine Repair?

7. _____

8. What was the total cost of the electronic typewriters?

8. _____

9. In which department is each of the electronic calculators located?

EC01 _____

EC02 _____

EC03 _____

10. When were the dot matrix printers purchased?

DP01 _____

DP02 _____

BONUS QUESTIONS

1. What is the average cost of all equipment in the inventory?

2. From which manufacturer were the most items of equipment purchased?

3. Prepare a pie chart showing the cost of the equipment in each of the three departments.

1. _____

2. _____

TASK 5
ADD RECORDS

Today, the data processing supervisor purchased two additional lap top computers, the first for the Production Department and the second for the Administration Department. Item CT08 has serial number DSCR73242, and item CT09 has serial number DSCR73278. Both were made by Teltek and will be serviced by City Computer Repair. Use today's date for date purchased. They cost $1,695 each, and their service expiration dates are three months from the first of next month. Leave the LAST SERVICE DATE field blank for these items. Make these additions to the database. Verify that these records have been added by answering the following questions. Hand in this answer sheet to your instructor.

1. How many items of equipment does the Production Department now have?

1. _____

2. How many items of equipment does the Administration Department now have?

2. _____

3. What was the total cost of the one old and two new lap top computers?

3. _____

4. How many items of equipment are now serviced by City Computer Repair?

4. _____

5. What is the total cost of the equipment now housed in the Production Department?

5. _____

TASK 6
DELETE RECORDS

The office supervisor has notified you that items AM01 and AM02, the answering machines, are being permanently taken out of service. Delete them from the file. Verify that the records have been deleted by answering the following questions. Hand in this answer sheet to your instructor.

1. How many items of equipment are now left in the Sales Department?

2. How many items of equipment are now left in the Administration Department?

3. What is the total cost of the equipment now housed in the Sales Department?

4. How many items of equipment are now serviced by Ace Machine Service?

5. What is the average cost of all items of equipment located in the Administration Department?

1. _____

2. _____

3. _____

4. _____

5. _____

TASK 7
MAKE CHANGES
IN RECORDS

Make the following changes, indicated in the list below, in the records contained in your inventory file. Write today's date in the blank beside each change to show that the change has been made. Then answer the questions below and hand in this answer sheet to your instructor.

1. A computer repairer from City Computer Repair has left a service report for a visit made today. Update the LAST SERVICE DATE field for these records: item codes CT07, CT08, and CT09. Use today's date.
    Change made on (date) _____.

2. You have received a memo from the computer supervisor that from now on City Computer Repair will no longer service any of our equipment. Instead, a new service contract has been signed with LDI, Inc., to do the work formerly done by City Computer Repair. Make the necessary changes in the file.
    Change made on (date) _____.

3. Items CB01 and PS01 have been transferred from the Administration Department to the Production Department. Change the computer file accordingly.
    Change made on (date) _____.

4. An error has been discovered in the serial number of item LP01. The number should be 275Q312. Correct the computer record for this item. Change made on (date) _____.

5. One of the manufacturers, Deltacorp, has been purchased by a larger company named Orbit Enterprises. Make the name change in the MANUFACTURER field for any items carrying the old Deltacorp name. Abbreviate the word *Enterprises* if necessary. Change made on (date) _____.

Answer the following after the above changes have been made.

1. How many items of equipment are now housed in the Production Department?

    1. _____

2. How many items of equipment are now housed in the Administration Department?

    2. _____

3. How many items of equipment can be serviced by the new service vendor LDI, Inc.?

    3. _____

4. What is the total value of the equipment serviced by LDI, Inc.?

    4. _____

5. What is the serial number of the laser printer?

    5. _____

TASK 8
ANSWER
INQUIRIES

Using your computer file, answer the following inquiries and write the answers on this answer sheet. Hand in the completed sheet to your instructor.

1. What is the item code of the most expensive item of equipment in the file?

    1. _____

2. What is the item name of the least expensive item of equipment in the file?

    2. _____

3. What is the item code of the item that was purchased most recently?

    3. _____

4. What is the item code of the item that has gone the longest time without service?

    4. _____

5. How much would it cost to purchase all of the leased equipment if the purchase price is the amount in the COST field?

    5. _____

6. What was the total cost of all purchased equipment in the file?

    6. _____

7. Which item codes have expiration dates in the month of September?

    7. _____

8. What are the item codes of equipment costing less than $400?

    8. _____

9. What are the item codes of equipment costing more than $1,000?

    9. _____

10. What is the average cost of equipment manufactured by Orbit Enterprises?

    10. _____

TASK 9
PRINT A LISTING
OF THE FILE

Sort the file by item code in ascending order. Then print a copy of the file, listing all data in every record. Then, reading from your hard copy, answer the following questions about the database. Hand in this answer sheet to your instructor.

1. How many items are in the database?

    1. _____

2. Who is the manufacturer for item CT02?

    2. _____

3. Who is the service vendor for item CT09?

    3. _____

4. What is the item name for item CT08?

    4. _____

5. Is item PS01 purchased or leased?

    5. _____

6. What is the expiration date for item EC02?

    6. _____

7. What is the cost of item QP01?

    7. _____

8. What was the last service date of the burster?

    8. _____

9. In what department is the paper shredder housed?

    9. _____

10. On what date was the letter quality printer purchased?

    10. _____

TASK 10
PREPARE A FOR-
MAL REPORT

The president of Hi-Tech wants a list of all equipment and its total value. Prepare a formal report for the president. Sort by department as the primary field and by item code as the secondary field, if your database program allows. Include the ITEM CODE, ITEM NAME, DEPARTMENT, DATE PURCHASED/LEASED, PURCHASED/LEASED, and COST fields. Compute and print the total cost of items by department, and compute and print a grand total. Use the following format for the report heading:

OFFICE EQUIPMENT INVENTORY

ITEM NO.　ITEM NAME　DEPT.　DATE OBTAINED　P/L　COST

Write the subtotals for each department and the grand total in the spaces below. Hand in this answer sheet and the report to your instructor.

Subtotal, Administration Department　　$ _____

Subtotal, Production Department　　$ _____

Subtotal, Sales Department　　$ _____

Grand Total, All Departments　　$ _____

HI-TECH FABRICATORS: EQUIPMENT INVENTORY LIST

Item Code	Item Name	Dept.	Date Purchased/ Leased	P/L	Expira- tion Date	Serial Number	Cost	Service Vendor	Last Service Date	Manufacturer
AM01	Answering machine	Sales	87/03/31	P	06/30	A45231M	239.00	Ace Machine Service	88/06/30	Teleco
AM02	Answering machine	Admin.	88/01/21	P	04/21	SEC4531	197.00	Ace Machine Service	88/01/21	Autofon
EC01	Electronic calculator	Prod.	88/01/10	P	01/10	BZ8760	179.00	Supra Machine Repair	88/04/19	E Z Key
EC02	Electronic calculator	Admin.	88/07/01	P	07/01	870CE43	179.00	Supra Machine Repair	89/07/16	E Z Key
EC03	Electronic calculator	Sales	88/01/15	P	01/15	ER342C2	179.00	Supra Machine Repair	88/06/20	Electrocom
ET01	Electronic typewriter	Admin.	86/06/30	P	06/30	984CTS	699.00	Best Key Service	89/09/27	Silktype
ET02	Electronic typewriter	Prod.	88/06/30	P	08/04	TR43C678	699.00	Best Key Service	88/07/24	Silktype
ET03	Electronic typewriter	Sales	87/08/15	P	01/15	XX434C412	439.00	Best Key Service	88/01/16	Horizon
PC01	Plain paper copier	Admin.	89/09/18	P	09/18	CZZX8720	1545.00	Venus Repair	89/10/01	Emperor
PC02	Plain paper copier	Sales	89/09/18	P	09/18	1298506CCA	495.00	Venus Repair	89/12/30	Superior
FM01	Facsimile machine	Admin.	88/05/12	P	05/12	FNI123X13	1499.00	Ace Machine Service	89/05/29	Fonfax
CM01	Computer modem	Admin.	87/07/01	P	07/01	E54CV63	590.00	Interstate Lines	88/07/31	Telmode
CM02	Computer modem	Sales	89/04/24	P	04/24	XXX534	390.00	Interstate Lines	89/05/21	Tecline
CP01	Computer processor	Admin.	88/07/01	L	07/01	PX847393	8500.00	City Computer Repair	89/01/13	Digiquip
CT01	Computer terminal	Admin.	88/07/01	L	07/01	66574DEY	499.00	City Computer Repair	89/09/22	Digiquip
CT02	Computer terminal	Admin.	88/07/01	L	07/01	665712DY	499.00	City Computer Repair	89/01/31	Digiquip
CT03	Computer terminal	Sales	88/07/01	L	07/01	678543DY	499.00	City Computer Repair	89/07/01	Digiquip
CT04	Computer terminal	Sales	88/07/01	L	07/01	672244DY	499.00	City Computer Repair	89/09/22	Digiquip
CT05	Computer terminal	Sales	88/07/01	L	07/01	693658DY	499.00	City Computer Repair	89/01/31	Digiquip
CT06	Computer terminal	Prod.	89/06/30	L	06/30	928477EE	400.00	City Computer Repair	89/06/30	Digiquip
CT07	Lap top computer	Sales	89/06/01	P	06/01	DCSRT3345	1800.00	City Computer Repair	89/06/01	Teltek
LP01	Laser printer	Admin.	89/05/15	P	05/15	4838CV346	2750.00	City Computer Repair	89/10/26	Ecoprint
DP01	Dot matrix printer	Sales	88/11/01	P	11/01	PNT9037	699.00	Venus Repair	89/03/17	Deltacorp
DP02	Dot matrix printer	Admin.	88/11/01	P	11/01	PNT8964	699.00	Venus Repair	89/11/01	Deltacorp
QP01	Letter quality printer.	Admin.	87/07/15	P	07/15	777345X	1179.00	City Computer Repair	89/07/15	Digiquip
CS01	Scanner	Sales	89/12/31	P	12/31	XZRT4563	639.00	City Computer Repair	89/12/31	Scantek
CB01	Burster	Admin.	87/08/29	P	08/29	111876CX	1479.00	Venus Repair	88/12/31	Echo
PS01	Paper shredder	Admin.	88/02/14	P	02/14	PMLDF666	369.00	Venus Repair	89/11/12	Deltacorp

GLOSSARY

alphanumeric field   A field which may contain any character—a letter of the alphabet, a digit (0–9), a symbol, or a punctuation mark. Also called a character field.

append   To add records to an existing file.

ascending sort   To arrange field entries in a–z or 0–9 order.

ASCII   American Standard Code for Information Interchange. The computer code used in most American computers for representing characters.

backup   A copy of data files and programs kept in case the original is damaged or lost.

browse   A database search in which the cursor is moved downward through selected records.

case sensitivity   A condition of differentiating between uppercase and lowercase letters.

coded field   A field entry made in abbreviated or very brief form. An example is F for *full-time student*.

columnar screen   A database screen format in which field names are aligned in a column at the left.

command-driven   A type of software in which the user must key in the option needed to create and maintain a database file. Software is either command-driven or menu-driven.

control break   A temporary change in a sort key in order to produce a subtotal or total.

data   Raw facts that can be used to produce information.

database   An orderly and usually very large body of information which allows the processing, accessing, and retrieval of that information. Also refers to a related group of files.

date field   A field that contains digits representing the year, month, and day.

DBMS (database management system) A computer program, or software package, that allows the creation and use of a database.

descending sort To arrange field entries in z–a or 9–0 order.

detail report A report that lists at least part of every record in the file.

document screen A database screen format in which field names appear in positions similar to the source document.

documentation A record of the design of a database. Also refers to user manuals accompanying commercial software.

---------------- **E** ----------------

exception report A report that lists only those records meeting a specified condition.

---------------- **F** ----------------

field An item of information in a record. For example, in an employee record one field might be social security number.

file A section of a database for a particular function, such as an employee file, an accounts receivable file, or a customer file.

file integrity Protecting computer information from damage and unauthorized use and ensuring that database information is accurate.

filename The caption used to identify a computer file.

---------------- **G** ----------------

graphics The software that is used to design graphs, charts, tables, and other illustrations.

---------------- **H** ----------------

hard copy Database information printed on paper.

help function A function in software that permits the operator to ask questions about database software during use. Answers appear on the screen.

hierarchical A database which organizes information in a tree-like structure by identifying each piece of data and defining the relationships among them.

hot line A telephone number, usually toll-free, which can be called for assistance concerning database software.

---------------- **I** ----------------

information Data that have been processed into useful form.

insert To place a new record between two existing records in a database file.

integrated software   Software that can perform two or more functions, such as database, spreadsheet, word processing, graphics, or communications.

————————— **K** —————————

key field   A field whose content is unique for each record in the file.

————————— **L** —————————

listing   An informal printout or screen display of records without formal titles or a special format.

logical deletion   A tentative removal of a database record, as distinguished from a physical deletion, which is final.

logical field   A field that may contain only a true/false or yes/no response.

logical view   How users view the data in a database.

————————— **M** —————————

memo field   A field that contains narrative information used only for reference or documentation.

menu-driven   A type of software that allows a user to select options from a list on the screen to create and maintain a database file. Software is either menu-driven or command-driven.

modular software   Software that is sold separately in independent components, such as word processing, database, spreadsheet, or graphics. The user buys only the component(s) needed and can easily combine components.

multiple search criteria   Facts about more than one characteristic used in a database search.

————————— **N** —————————

network database   A database model similar to hierarchical that is used most often with large computer systems. Network databases are complex in structure.

numeric field   A field containing only digits (0–9), a decimal point (optional), and a minus sign (optional).

————————— **P** —————————

password   A secret code or name, known only by authorized users of a computer database, which permits access to the system.

physical deletion   A permanent removal of a database record. Once the record is physically deleted, it is irretrievable. (See also logical deletion.)

physical view   The way in which data are actually arranged in a database.

primary key The field that is consulted first when retrieving a record. Distinguished from secondary key, which would be consulted if the primary key is not known.

primary sort key Also known as major sort key, it is used for main headings in a sorted database listing or report. Distinguished from secondary sort key, also known as minor sort key, which is used for subheadings in a sorted database listing or report.

_____ **R** _____

record One item in a file representing a person, product, or other unit. For example, in an employee file the information about one employee is a record.

relational database The database model most often used with microcomputers. Requires fixed-length records and fields.

relational operator A command specifying the logic of a database search.

report A formal hard-copy printout of records in a specific format.

_____ **S** _____

search criteria Facts about database records to be retrieved.

secondary key The field that is used to retrieve a record only when the primary key is unknown.

secondary sort key Also known as minor sort key, this key is used for subheadings in a sorted database listing or report. (See also primary sort key.)

self-documenting Term used to describe a filename that identifies a file.

sequential record search Looking through records in a database from beginning to end.

sorted records Records in a certain sequence or order.

source document A form (such as a sales receipt, employee form, or packing slip) from which a database record is designed.

spreadsheet The software that is used to perform calculations.

summary report A report that lists only subtotals and totals from the records in a database.

_____ **T** _____

template A piece of plastic or cardboard that fits over the function keys on the computer keyboard to label the function of each key.

truncate   To cut off the first few digits in a numeric field entry or the last few characters in an alphanumeric field entry because of the limited size of the field.

tutorial   An instructional program, usually on disk, which accompanies some commercial software.

_____ **U** _____

undelete   To recover a record which has been logically but not physically deleted.

update   To add, delete, and change database records.

user-friendly   A factor used in evaluating database software. Relates to whether software is easy to learn as well as menu- or command-driven.

_____ **W** _____

wild card   A character that can be used in a computer search to take the place of any character in the file.

word processing software   The software that is used to create and edit text.

KEY TO SELF-CHECK REVIEW QUESTIONS

CHAPTER 1

True or False
1. T
2. F *Information, not data.*
3. F *File, not field.*
4. T
5. T
6. T
7. F *Cannot contain # sign.*
8. F *It is either a numeric or alphanumeric field; REORDER POINT is not a question answerable by Yes/No or True/False.*
9. F *Typically dates are 6 digits—mmddyy or yymmdd.*
10. T
11. T

Multiple Choice
1. c
2. a
3. b
4. d
5. c
6. a
7. b
8. a
9. d
10. c

CHAPTER 2

True or False
1. T
2. T
3. F *This is a logical field, answerable by Yes/No or True/False.*
4. F *Needs 6 digits; (i.e., 050589).*
5. T
6. F *Different departments have different uses and needs for data.*
7. F *The most important consideration for a key field is that it be a unique identifier for the record.*
8. T
9. T
10. T
11. F *Proofreading is always important during data entry as it will save problems later.*
12. F *Being consistent in using all upper or lowercase on sort fields is important because the same letter sorts differently depending on case; i.e., the computer treats B and b as separate and different characters.*

Multiple Choice
1. b
2. d
3. b
4. b
5. d
6. c
7. d
8. b
9. a
10. b

CHAPTER 3

True or False
1. T
2. T
3. T
4. F *Since the primary key is unique to one record, only one record should be retrieved.*
5. F *Often the secondary key is not unique, so it is possible several records will be retrieved.*
6. F *Command-driven databases do not use menus; the user types in a command.*
7. T
8. T
9. F *Relational operators are $=$, $>$, $<$. Wild card refers to a character that can take the place of any character during a search.*

10. F *Logically deleted means the record is merely flagged for deletion; physically deleted means the record is actually removed.*
11. F *Unless you make and retain a hard copy of the record before changing it, the record is permanently altered in the database.*
12. T
13. F *Once physically deleted, the record is gone.*
14. T

Multiple Choice
1. b
2. d
3. a
4. c
5. b
6. d
7. c
8. a
9. b
10. d

Short Answer
1. search criteria
2. relational operators
3. multiple
4. wild card
5. appending
6. logically
7. physically
8. menu driven
9. undelete
10. browse

Using Relational Operators
1. a
2. e, f, g
3. a
4. c, f
5. a, e
6. none
7. c, d, f

CHAPTER 4

True or False
1. T
2. F *Both can be sorted in either ascending or descending order.*

3. F *Warehouse location is the primary sort key; description is secondary.*
4. T
5. F *A separate sorted file needs a different name; using the same name will cause the original file to be erased.*
6. F *A separate sorted file is not automatically updated.*
7. T
8. F *The opposite is true.*
9. T
10. F *Case sensitivity means the computer is sensitive to (treats differently) uppercase and lowercase letters.*
11. F *Both can create reports having subtotals and totals.*
12. T

Multiple Choice
1. b
2. d
3. b
4. b
5. c
6. d
7. a
8. c
9. b
10. c

CHAPTER 5

True or False
1. T
2. F *File integrity refers to protection and accuracy of the data in the file.*
3. F *Keeping a backup is important because the data are valuable.*
4. F *Backups should be kept separate from originals in case of disaster.*
5. T
6. F *Only data in the computer's memory is lost, not that on disk.*
7. T
8. F *Proofreading is necessary; computers cannot proofread.*
9. T
10. T
11. F *Selective access is achieved through the use of various passwords.*
12. T
13. T

14. T

15. F *There are limits to what can be copied; some packages do not use ASCII.*

Multiple Choice

1. b
2. a
3. d
4. c
5. c
6. a
7. d
8. d
9. b
10. c

INDEXING RULES

Names must be entered into databases in a standard format. The following indexing rules are guidelines for such standardization.

Rule 1 Names of Persons

When indexing the name of a person, arrange the units in this order: last name, first name or initial, and middle name or initial.

Rule 2 Personal Names With Prefixes

Consider a prefix, such as *Mc* in *McDonald*, as part of the name it precedes. Ignore any apostrophe or space that appears within or after the prefix.

Commonly used prefixes are *d', D', de, De, Del, De la, Di, Du, El, Fitz, La, Le, M, Mac, Mc, O', Saint, St., Van, Van de, Van der, Von,* and *Von der*.

Rule 3 Hyphenated Personal Names

Consider a hyphenated first, middle, or last name as one unit.

Rule 4 Abbreviations of Personal Names

Abbreviated and shortened forms of personal names are indexed as written.

Rule 5 Personal Names With Titles and Suffixes

When used with a person's name, a title or a suffix is the last indexing unit when needed to distinguish between two or more identical names. Titles and suffixes are indexed as written.

Titles include *Capt., Dr., Mayor, Miss, Mr., Mrs., Ms.,* and *Senator.* Suffixes include seniority terms *(III, Jr., Sr.)* and professional designations *(CPA, M.D., Ph.D.).*

Note: Numeric seniority terms (II, III) are filed before alphabetic terms (Jr., Sr.)

Rule 6   Names of Businesses and Organizations

Consider the units in business and organization names in the order in which they are normally written. To determine the order in which a business or organization name is normally written, use the letterhead of the business or organization. If the letterhead is not available, use such alternate sources as directories, advertisements, and computer databases. However, when *The* is the first word of the name, it is treated as the last unit. Names with prefixes are considered one unit, just as with personal names.

Rule 7   Abbreviations in Business and Organization Names

Abbreviations in business and organization names are indexed as written.

Note: Cross-reference between an abbreviation and the complete name when necessary to ensure that records can be located.

Rule 8   Punctuation in Business and Organization Names

Ignore any punctuation marks that appear in business and organization names. Just as with personal names, hyphenated business and organization names are treated as one unit.

Punctuation marks include the apostrophe, colon, comma, dash, exclamation point, hyphen, parentheses, period, question mark, quotation marks, and semicolon.

Rule 9   Numbers in Business and Organization Names

Arabic numerals (2, 17) and Roman numerals (II, IV) are considered one unit and are filed in numeric order before alphabetic characters. All Arabic numerals precede all Roman numerals. Hyphenated numbers (7-11) are indexed according to the number before the hyphen (7); the number after the hyphen (11) is ignored. The letters *st, d,* and *th* following an Arabic numeral are ignored. Thus 1st is indexed as 1; 2nd as 2; and 4th as 4.

If a number in a business or organization name is spelled out (*First* Street Pizza), it is filed alphabetically as written. Hyphenated numbers that are spelled out (*Twenty-One* Restaurant) are considered one unit (*TWENTYONE* RESTAURANT). An Arabic numeral followed by a hyphen and a word (7-Gable) is considered one unit (7GABLE).

Rule 10   Symbols in Business and Organization Names

If a symbol is part of a name, the symbol is indexed as if spelled out, as shown here:

Symbol	*Indexed As*
&	AND
¢	CENT or CENTS
$	DOLLAR or DOLLARS
#	NUMBER or POUNDS
%	PERCENT

Note: If the $ sign is used with a number, file first under the number.

Rule 11   Government Names

Government names are indexed first by the name of the country, state, county, or city. The distinctive name of the department, bureau, or board is considered next. United States federal government names are indexed first under *United States Government*.

Rule 12   Addresses

When names are otherwise identical, they may be filed by address. The elements of the address are considered in the following order: city, state, street name, and house or building number.

Note: The house or building number is considered in numeric order.

INDEX

Abbreviations, indexing of:
  in business names, 82
  in personal names, 81
Accounting functions, integrated software for, 63–64
Adding records, 38, 60
Addresses, indexing of, 83
Alphabetic sorting, 45, 46, 50, 52
Alphabetic filing rules (see Indexing rules)
Alphanumeric field, 8–10, 20
American Standard Code for Information Interchange (ASCII), 24, 48–49, 65
Appending records, 38
Ascending sort, 45, 46
ASCII (American Standard Code for Information Interchange), 24, 48–49, 65

Backup data disk, 60
Browse, 35, 37
Business names, indexing of, 82
  with abbreviations, 82
  with numbers, 82
  with punctuation, 82
  with symbols, 83

Case sensitivity, 24, 48
Changing records, 39, 60
Character field, 9
Coded field, 19–20, 23, 31
Coding scheme, 48
Columnar screen, 22
Command-driven DBMS, 33, 34
Communication program, 63
Compatibility of software packages, 65
Computer lock, 61
Computer program (see Software packages)

Data, 1, 3
  database design and, 15
  database entering, 23–24
  organization of, 1–2
  in relational database, 11
  saving, 59–60
  sorting, 24
  versus information, 4
Database, 2, 7–9
  access levels, 60
  components, 7–9

  creation of, 6–7
  hierarchical, 11
  information and, 6
  network, 11
  organization, 11
  relational, 11
Database design, 6–7, 16–23
  coded field, 19–20, 23, 31
  columnar screen, 22
  data and, 15
  data proofreading, 24–25
  documentation, 16, 23
  document screen, 22, 23
  field and, 16–22
  field names, 16, 19
  field sequencing, 16, 21–22
  filename, 16, 17
  key field, 16–18
  logical view, 15
  physical view, 16
  record and, 16
  record entry, 23–24
Database management system (see DBMS)
Database screen, 22, 23
Database software, 6, 62–64
Date field, 8, 9, 20
dBase (Ashton Tate), 48
DBMS (database management system), 6, 29
  command-driven, 33, 34
  file updating with, 38–39
  menu-driven, 34, 35
  record locating with, 30–38
  record sorting with, 45–48
  report producing with, 49–51
  security and, 60
Deleting records, 38–39, 60
  logically deleted, 38
  physically deleted, 38
  undelete feature, 38–39
Descending sort, 45, 47
Detail report, 49, 50, 54
DIF (Data Interchange Format), 65
Disk:
  backup, 60
  maintenance, 61
  storage, 60, 61
Document screen, 22, 23
Documentation, 16, 23
  of report, 54